HARDPRESS.NET
HOME OF HARD-TO-FIND BOOKS

An Historical Account of the Orphan Hospital of Edinburgh ...

by Orphan Hospital and Workhouse at Edinburgh

AN

HISTORICAL ACCOUNT

OF

THE ORPHAN HOSPITAL

OF

EDINBURGH.

**DRAWN UP AND PRINTED BY DESIRE OF THE
MANAGERS.**

EDINBURGH:
PRINTED BY J. AND C. MUIRHEAD.

1833.

-2878

TO

THE RIGHT HONOURABLE

CHARLES HOPE,

LORD PRESIDENT OF THE COURT OF SESSION,

PRESES OF THE INCORPORATION OF

THE ORPHAN HOSPITAL

OF

EDINBURGH,

THIS

HISTORICAL ACCOUNT OF THE INSTITUTION

IS MOST RESPECTFULLY INSCRIBED.

OFFICE-BEARERS,
ELECTED, 12TH AUGUST, 1833.

PRESES OF THE INCORPORATION,
THE RIGHT HONOURABLE CHARLES HOPE,
LORD PRESIDENT OF THE COURT OF SESSION.

MANAGERS.
JOHN S. MORE, Advocate.
Sir HENRY JARDINE.
JOHN ELDER, W. S.
WALTER DICKSON, W. S.
Rev. T. S. JONES, D. D.
Rev. ROBERT GORDON, D. D.
JOHN ABERCROMBIE, Physician.
Rev. DAVID RITCHIE, D. D.
ROBERT PLENDERLEATH, Merchant.
Sir JOHN STUART FORBES, Bart.
ANDREW TAWSE, W. S.
WILLIAM YOUNG, W. S.
W. P. ALISON, Physician.
ROBERT BELL, Advocate.
WILLIAM PAUL, Accountant.

ROBERT PAUL, *Treasurer.*
WM. SCOTT MONCREIFF, *Accountant.*
JOHN TAWSE, *Comptroller.*
JAMES & WALTER JOLLIE, *Clerks.*
WILLIAM BROWN, *Surgeon.*

JOHN RITCHIE, *House-Governor and Teacher.*
JANET SINCLAIR, *Matron.*
JANE PANTON, *Female Teacher.*

HISTORICAL ACCOUNT, &c.

THE ORPHAN HOSPITAL has now for a century held a prominent place among the Charitable Institutions of the Metropolis of Scotland, and its utility has been very generally acknowledged. But it appears to be of importance, at the present time, to offer a somewhat more enlarged account than has hitherto been published of its origin, progress, and history; and of the circumstances which induce the Managers to submit these to public consideration.

The Institution originated in the active benevolence of an individual citizen, Mr. Andrew Gairdner, merchant in Edinburgh. In the year 1727, he was Treasurer of the Trinity Hospital, an Institution founded in 1461 by Mary of Gueldres, consort to King James the Second, as a refuge for decayed burgesses; and, finding the fabric of that house to be in a dilapidated state, he opened a subscription for the purpose of repairing it. Having his attention by some means turned, at the same time, to the number of orphan children in Edinburgh and other parts of Scotland, who were left in very destitute circumstances, and exposed to all the evils inseparable from a state of idleness and ignorance, he resolved to combine with the subscriptions for the Trinity Hospital the formation of a fund for erecting an Orphan Institution. With this view he published two treatises, the one entitled, " A Looking-glass for Rich People, or a Plea for the Poor," the other, a reprint of a foreign work, entitled " Pietas Hallensis, " or a History of the Orphan House at Glauca in Saxony, " by A. H. Frank, Professor of Divinity in the University of " Halle," which he intended to be the model of the proposed Institution.

By his exertions Mr. Gairdner collected for these objects above One Thousand Pounds, and, after repairing the Trinity

Hospital, he set aside the balance of £218 : 13 : 5d. as a fund for the benefit of orphans.

The proposal was first communicated to the Society in Scotland for Propagating Christian Knowledge, from whom it received great encouragement, and under whose superintendence a constitution was framed for the Hospital; and in September 1733, a house in Bailie Fife's Close, belonging to Mr. Trotter of Morton, was hired at the rent of £12 per annum; furniture procured to the value of £15; thirty children selected and admitted; and Mr. George Brown, one of the teachers of the Society for Propagating Christian Knowledge at the Bridge of Kelty, near Dunblane, chosen master, whose salary the Society agreed to pay, as well as to furnish books for the children.

From one of the pamphlets published by Mr. Gairdner, it would appear that his mind was much impressed with the importance of promoting in his native city the manufacture of woollen and linen cloths, which he thought had been greatly neglected. Combining with this object the duty of rearing the orphans to habits of industry, he induced the Managers to purchase from the Town of Edinburgh a considerable share of the lease of Paul's Work, which had formerly been a religious house, but was now converted into a woollen and linen manufactory. In this place a great proportion of the orphan boys were trained to the weaving business; but in the course of time so many difficulties and disadvantages were found to be inseparable from the scheme, that it was ultimately abandoned, and the lease given up.

In the year 1734, a general collection was made in all the churches and meeting-houses of the city, as well as in several country parishes, in behalf of the Institution; from which so liberal a sum was obtained, that Mr. Gairdner and his friends were enabled to feu a piece of ground called *The Dingwall Park*, belonging to the Trinity Hospital, and immediately adjoining the Trinity College Church; and having received a plan from Mr. William Adam, the most eminent architect of his time, they commenced the erection of a suitable building for an Hospital, the foundation of which was laid on the 28th June in that year. As a proof of the general feeling that prevailed in favour of the infant Institution, it may here be noticed, that twenty-four journeymen wrights voluntarily signed a paper, engaging to work gratuitously in the erection of the house for one hundred and forty days,—the candlemakers of Edinburgh sent in a subscription paper, binding themselves to give to the Hospital annually the quantities of candles annexed to their names, amounting to thirteen stones;—and a person who desired his name not to be known, caused a frontispiece in marble to be prepared in London, with a suitable inscription, bearing the date of the founding of the Hospital, and to be put up above the principal entry to the house.*

In 1735 the children were removed to the new building which had been prepared for their reception; and, about the same time, the Lord Provost, Magistrates, and Council granted a Seal of Cause to the Hospital, which continued to receive regular accessions to its funds by individual subscriptions, by considerable legacies, and by collections made within the bounds of the Presbytery and some of the Synods of the Church, as well as those received on the evenings of the Sabbath, when the children were regularly catechised in the house, and where great numbers of the citizens appear to have attended. So that, in 1739, when Mr. Gairdner died, there were seventy-four orphans maintained and educated in the Institution, and a part of its stock had, by that time, been invested in the purchase of land in the neighbourhood of Inveresk.

In 1742, by the good services of the Marquis of Tweeddale, then Secretary of State, the Institution received the countenance and favour of Government, his Majesty George II. having been graciously pleased to grant Royal Letters Patent, erecting certain contributors and others into a Corporation, and conferring upon them all the necessary powers for managing the Charity; in pursuance of which the Corporation proceeded to frame a set of Statutes or Bye-Laws for the regulation of its concerns, and which, being afterwards amended and renewed in the year 1776, form, along with the Charter, the constitution by which the Hospital has ever since been governed. A copy of the Charter and Bye-Laws will be found in the Appendix, Nos. 1 and 2.

* As an illustration of the same spirit at an after period, it may be mentioned, that it is recorded in the year 1777, that " Dr. Glen, Phy-" sician in Edinburgh, presented a Clock to the Hospital; John Young " gave the Dial-plate; John Bonar painted it; and Thomas M'Innes " put it up."

By one of these laws the individuals constituting the Corporation were authorised to assume into their body any individuals who, from time to time, should become donors to the Institution. An entire list of the original members, of those nominated by the patent, and of all who have been assumed to the present time, is also given in the Appendix, No. 3. In this list, some who do, and others who do not yet belong to the Incorporation, will recognise the names of their fathers and forefathers, and of many of the most honourable and respectable members of the community.

Previous to the year 1743, there was no such institution in Edinburgh as the City Charity Workhouse, and a considerable proportion of those who were admitted to the benefits of the Orphan Hospital were, therefore, the children of parents who belonged to the city, and had been domiciled there. On this account the chief source of its steady revenue consisted in the collections which were annually made in its behalf in the several parish churches and places of worship in the city and neighbourhood. But when, in the above year, the Charity Workhouse was erected, these collections were discontinued, and the admission of children to the Hospital was accordingly so much restricted, that, in 1748, there were only thirty in the house.

The minds of the Managers, however, seem to have been intent on giving to the Institution a wider sphere of operation than had hitherto been embraced by it, and, on rendering its advantages accessible to those children from all parts of the kingdom, who, in the course of Providence, might be left orphans and destitute, and bereft of every other resource for their support and education, and their moral and religious discipline.

These intentions were greatly promoted, and the means of fulfilling them provided, by the labours of that distinguished individual, the Rev. George Whitfield, who, by the frequent sermons preached in the course of the summer evenings in the park to the east and south of the Hospital, and which were continued, at different intervals, from 1741 down to 1768, procured collections in its behalf to the amount of £1592. These sermons were attended by a great number of pious persons from the city and neighbourhood, who obtained permission to erect seats or sheds in the park for their own accommodation, the materials of which were afterwards sold for the benefit of the Hospital, and, in one year, produced the sum of £80. The Institution was also greatly indebted to the Rev. Joseph Townsend, Rector of Pewsey, in Wiltshire, who, by preaching in the Hospital Park for some months in the years 1767, 1768, and 1769, raised upwards of £400, and, to many other clergymen at home, as well as from England, who, by the same means, contributed to augment its funds.

Nor ought the obligations of the Hospital at this time to other individuals be forgotten, who, in a different way, endeavoured to promote the same object. Even from the year 1739, the free proceeds of the Ladies' Concerts and Assemblies in Edinburgh were not unfrequently devoted to this purpose, and, in 1745, it is recorded, that the Lady Orbiston, the only surviving Directrix of the Edinburgh Assembly, made over to the Hospital " The whole gear and plenishing " of the Assembly Hall," the attendance at which had probably been discontinued in consequence of the public commotions of that memorable year.

Considerable legacies and donations continued to be given from time to time to the Institution, among which it is not uninteresting to notice an early benefaction from the well-known Colonel Gardner, a subscription in 1754 among the Liverymen of London, and, a considerable number of years afterwards, a donation of £150 from the Authors of the " Mirror," by the hands of Henry Mackenzie, Esq.* From these and various other sources, such a sum was collected as enabled the Managers to place the Institution on a firm foundation. And as, with a view to this, a regulation had been made that all donations above £5, unless specially directed otherwise, should be converted into stock, and not considered as forming any part of the ordinary revenue which could be annually expended for the support of the Charity, so, in the course of time, a respectable capital came to be accumulated, a considerable part of which was invested in the purchase of the farms of Greenlaw and Holyrig in the county of Berwick.

The discipline and occupation of the children appear from the beginning to have been watched over with great solicitude by the Managers, particularly the instilling into their minds

* A list of all donations and legacies to the Institution, which amounted to £10 and upwards, will be found in the Appendix, No. 4. and those are pointed out by which a right of presentation was established.

the principles of religion, and the training them to habits of
industry. When Mr. Brown, the first Master of the house,
resigned his situation, being called by a congregation of
Protestant Dissenters in England to be their Pastor, the
office was for some time filled by Mr. Francis Archibald, who
had formerly been Minister of the parish of Guthrie; and in
the year 1759, the Managers were most providentially led to
secure the services of an individual in the internal superintendence of the Institution, of whom it is, perhaps, not too
much to say, that within his own sphere, and in his own day,
he was one of the most useful and valuable characters in the
city of Edinburgh. This was the late Mr. William Peebles.
He was originally brought into notice by a letter from Mr.
Thomas Randall, then Minister of Inchture, and father of the
late Dr. Davidson of Edinburgh, addressed to Mr. Archibald
Wallace, one of the Managers, in which he says,—" Having
" observed some time ago an advertisement in the newspapers
" from the Orphan Hospital concerning a Schoolmaster to
" the children there, I give you this trouble in regard there is
" one William Peebles who, I think, comes precisely up to the
" description of the one wanted by you for that end. For of
" him, I think, I am at liberty to testify, if of any in the world,
" that he is born of God, and conscientious to the highest de-
" gree of scruple as to fulfilling whatever is committed to his
" charge. At present he is Schoolmaster at Strathmartine, a
" small parish, and of small encouragement, in this county,
" but of such reputation for teaching, and, particularly, for
" instilling the principles of religion into the youth under
" his care, that many from different parishes resort to him on
" this account. Content with what he has, he is willing to
" remain where he is, yet humbly rejoiced when I mentioned
" to him, which was necessary, my intention of writing to
" you on this head. I may justly add, that he is of the least
" meddling nature that can be. If things go well with his
" own soul, and well with those that are under his charge,
" he rests fully satisfied. I should say, that he teaches
" nothing but English, writing, and figuring,—his hand-
" writing is substantial and good; he understands well the
" different parts of arithmetic, and having naturally good
" parts, he is apt to learn any thing with ease; nor does he
" want an ear, if that were needful."
The excellent person thus suggested to the Managers, was
immediately chosen to be Master of the Institution, and for

nearly half a century continued to discharge the duties of his place with a degree of judgment, fidelity, and success, which, perhaps, more than any other circumstance, gave to the Orphan Hospital that character for substantial usefulness which it undoubtedly acquired, and which is still remembered by not a few of those who were trained under its roof. Nor can the superior qualities which, in every respect, belonged to Mr. Peebles be forgotten by any of the Managers of the Institution who live to recollect them, or by those who, otherwise unconnected with the Hospital, were in the practice, under various circumstances, of repairing to Mr. Peebles for counsel, guidance, and encouragement. For, during a long period of his life, the room of this good man was the frequent resort of some of the best and worthiest of the citizens, as well as of many young men who were prosecuting their studies at the University with a view to the sacred Ministry, and who, attracted by the singular talent which he possessed for religious conversation, the simplicity and godly sincerity of his character, and by the kind and affectionate manner in which he entered into all their employments and prospects, found in the matured knowledge and experience of Mr. Peebles the means of much personal improvement. Of these persons, after having been useful, and some of them eminent in their day, the greater part have been removed from the present life; but some yet remain in various quarters of the country. ——So ample a reference to the character of an individual may perhaps be considered as a digression. But it may not be without its use to hold forth such an example of private fidelity and unostentatious usefulness; at any rate, it seems not more than is due to the memory of one, with whose quiet labours in the retreat of a Charitable Institution for nearly the half of the period of its existence, a great part of those blessings is incorporated, which it has been the acknowledged instrument of diffusing.——Mr. Peebles died in 1807, and the Managers erected a tablet to his memory in the Schoolroom of the Hospital, with an inscription, written at their request by the Rev. Dr. Dickson, of St. Cuthbert's, of which a copy will be found in the Appendix, No. 5.

It is a circumstance not unworthy of remark, that in the mind of the individual who projects, or in the associations of those who are engaged in conducting one scheme of benevolence or christian usefulness, other plans for the public good have not unfrequently been germinated and matured. The original idea of the Orphan Hospital, as has already been noticed, occurred to Mr. Gairdner while he was prosecuting the objects of the Trinity Hospital; and effect was given to his views by the consultations that were held at the Board of the Society for Propagating Christian Knowledge. In a few years afterwards, a scheme for the relief of indigent incurables originated among the Managers of the Orphan Hospital; and again, in 1765, one of their number submitted to them a plan for the erection of a chapel on the Orphan House ground. This proposal proceeded upon the felt insufficiency of the accommodation which was furnished, even at that time, by the existing parish churches of the city, for the inhabitants who were in communion with the Established Church; and it was urged that the Managers should countenance the design and concur with those who were desirous of promoting it, not only with a view to the general advantage of the community, but also for the special benefit of the Hospital, the funds of which would be permanently augmented by the ground-rent of the chapel, and a portion of the collections, which it was intended should be expressly appropriated to this purpose.

The scheme was not immediately carried into effect; but, in a few years, the suggestion was taken up and acted upon by Lady Glenorchy, who, in August 1772, gave in a proposal to the Managers for feuing part of their ground for the erection of a Chapel at her own expense; in which her Ladyship stated, that she had the interests of the Hospital much at heart,—that she thought they would be materially promoted by the execution of her plan, if the Managers approved of it,—and that she would wish the Clergyman that might be settled in the chapel to take the ministerial charge of the children and servants of the Hospital. The purpose of Lady Glenorchy was accomplished; a place of worship was erected on a part of the Hospital's ground, in which many collections were made in its behalf, and from which, in a variety of other ways, much good has accrued to the Institution, as well as manifold blessings to multitudes of immortal men. And it is worthy of being here recorded, that, in fine keeping with his character among those who know and can appreciate it, the esteemed and venerable Pastor of the congregation of Lady Glenorchy's Chapel, Dr. Jones, has ever since the year 1779, when he entered upon his Ministry in that place, been one of the most true and steady friends of the Orphan Hospital, whilst he now stands the senior on the list of the living Members of the Incorporation.

In the year 1774, the first annual sermon for the Hospital was preached by the Rev. Dr. Erskine, which was afterwards published ;* and a fresh impulse appears to have been given to the cause of the Institution, if one may judge by the number of private subscriptions which were given to its funds. About the same period, in addition to a few that had been before established, several new presentations were founded by charitable individuals, who, upon the gift of specific sums, obtained a right in favour of themselves, or of certain nominees in all time coming, of presenting children to be received into the Hospital, provided that in all respects their circumstances were such as to have rendered them eligible without such right.

In the year last mentioned (1774), and during the time that the affairs of the Hospital were superintended by the late Mr. Scott Moncreiff of Newhalls, whose activity and zeal for a long course of years contributed greatly to the prosperity of the Institution,† the Managers resolved to make an addition to the House, by which it was rendered more commodious and healthy. A few years afterwards, the whole building then erected was found to be still too small for the increasing number of children, and accordingly, in 1781, it was resolved to complete the original plan of the fabric, the spire being added in 1783 ; and in 1787 an extension of the original plan was agreed on, and was carried into effect by the addition of the wings to the east and west of the house, the means of accomplishing which, as well as of adding a variety of improvements in order to give prominency and effect to the building, were provided for chiefly by the assiduity of Mr. Thomas Tod, then Treasurer to the Institution, who devoted the greater part of his energies and time to its concerns, and appears to have found in his attention to them the highest personal gratification and enjoyment. At his own request, his remains were deposited in the burying place appropriated to the Orphans.‡

* A list of the Clergymen who have preached the Annual Sermons will be found in the Appendix, No. 6.

† A list of the different Office-Bearers of the Institution, from its commencement to the present time, is given in the Appendix, No. 7.

‡ Besides several other publications in behalf of the Hospital, Mr. Tod published, in 1783, a Vindication of this and of other Charitable Institutions in Edinburgh, against the strictures of Dr. M'Farlan, one of

As an example of the industrious habits in which the children were trained,—and which, together with the cheerfulness and contentment that reigned among them, seem particularly to have arrested the attention of Mr. Howard, the philanthropist, during his frequent visits to the Hospital, a few years previous to the date now referred to, and which are specially noticed in the history of his benevolent travels throughout Europe,—it may be mentioned, that in 1789, when there were one hundred and forty children in the house, the following is the Report of the work performed by them during the preceding year :—

" The girls spun as much yarn as produced 500 yards of
" linen cloth, which they have made into shirts, &c. for the
" whole family. They made all their own gowns, and other
" apparel, assisted in washing and dressing the linens, served
" by turns in the kitchen, and kept the house clean. The
" youngest girls made as much lace as produced £10, which
" sum kept the whole family in sheets and blankets. The
" boys spun as much yarn as made 430 yards of woollen
" stuff for working dresses to themselves and the girls.
" As tailors, they made and mended all their own clothes.
" As shoemakers, they made and mended the hospital shoes.
" And, as bookbinders, they bound all their own books : and
" the boys and girls together knit 300 pairs of stockings." A similar degree of industry is exhibited by the ⸢statements of succeeding years.

There were circumstances in the state of the country towards the close of the last, and at the commencement of the present century, and which must still be in the recollection of many, that created a great pressure upon the funds of the Orphan Hospital, in common with those of almost every other charitable institution. The general distress which prevailed among the poorer classes of society, from the high price of provisions, and the number of those children whose fathers had fallen in defence of their country, that were thus left fatherless and destitute, increased the applica-

the Ministers of Canongate, who, although fully admitting the principle and objects of the Orphan Hospital to be unexceptionable, and to be distinguished in his opinion from those of many other charities, had, nevertheless, indulged in some gloomy anticipations as to its permanent advantages, arising from the indifference, selfishness, and cupidity with which its affairs might come to be administered,—anticipations which, it is gratifying to know, have never hitherto been realised.

tions for admission to an extent that had previously been unknown. And it is satisfactory to reflect, that the Managers were enabled to meet this emergency; for their records show, that, in 1799, forty-seven children were admitted; in the year following, fifty-three; and sixty-four in 1801; and that for the five years preceding 1804 two hundred and twenty children in all had been received into the house, a great proportion of whom, from all parts of the country, were the orphans of those who, to employ the language of the eloquent sermon preached for the Hospital, in 1801, by the late Mr. Bennet of Duddingstone, " had shed their blood abroad for " our peace and security at home, while we, sitting secure un- " der our vine and fig-tree, only heard the echoes of the dis- " tant war in faint and reverberated reports." The exertions thus made were owing very much to the judgment and Christian benevolence of Mr. Alexander Bonar, who held the office of Treasurer for eleven years previous to 1807, and who, by his disinterested labours during that period, rendered the most essential services to the Institution, and continued to the end of his life one of its warmest supporters and best friends.

In 1804 the Managers found, that by acting on the resolution of adding every donation above Five Pounds to the capital, their funds had gradually accumulated so as to enable them to make a farther investment in land by the purchase of the farm of Quixwood, in Berwickshire. And a few years afterwards, their hands were greatly strengthened by the accession of some considerable sums, the history of one or two of which may not be uninteresting.

When in the course of the anniversary sermon, in 1774, Dr. Erskine took occasion, while speaking of the Providence that watches over the lot of the orphan and fatherless, to ask, " Is there not a wheel within a wheel which sometimes " raises men of the meanest descent to useful and important " stations," no one was aware that an exemplification of this truth would, to a certain extent, be furnished in the case of an individual, who, nearly forty years before, had been educated and maintained in the Institution for which the Doctor was then pleading, who, in all probability lost sight of by every individual that had known the circumstances of his early years, was then pursuing his course of life in distant countries, and the development of whose history should not take place for thirty years still to come! Yet so it was.

In 1736, Richard Douglas, aged eight years, who had lost both his parents, was admitted into the Hospital on the recommendation of the Presbytery of Linlithgow. Three years afterwards, application was made to have him taken out of the Institution at the desire of his uncle, a merchant in Cadiz, who, it was stated, wished to support and educate him at his own expense. The Managers appear at first to have hesitated in granting this request, and not to have done so without obtaining security that the boy should be properly looked after and provided for. What immediately took place does not appear from the records of the Hospital, farther than that having in the year 1739 been removed from it under the circumstances now mentioned, in order to be sent to a friend abroad, he had accordingly gone, but not finding him, had returned, and being represented to be very destitute, the Managers waived a general rule of the Institution and in 1742 again received him into the house, where he remained till his education was completed; after which he was put to service.

Having entered into the Royal Navy, it is known that in 1757 he became Master's-mate, and in 1760 had attained the rank of Lieutenant; and, after passing a long life in the toils and duties of his profession, he returned and took up his residence in Edinburgh, where he continued till his death, much respected by the circle of friends to whom he was known. During this period he paid frequent visits to the Hospital, and gave occasional donations to its funds, in consequence of which he was assumed a Member of the Incorporation in 1799. It was not, however, till after his death, which took place a few years subsequent to this time, that it was discovered that he had been an early inmate of the Hospital, but having died intestate, though in possession of a considerable fortune, which in consequence fell to the Crown, the Managers, having from some accidental circumstances* been led to investigate his history, were enabled satisfactorily to trace his early connection with the Institution. And upon a representation of the facts, and of the reasonableness of the supposition that to the good principles which he had imbibed

* One of these was—Mr. Peebles happening to recollect that Mr. Douglas had been very minute in his inquiries respecting the Hospital during his visits to it, and on one occasion, while going through the house, had stopped in one of the rooms, and looking earnestly into the corner of it, said, " *There* have I slept many a night."

while under its charge he owed, by the divine blessing, all his success in life, the Barons of Exchequer were pleased, in 1810, to award about one-fifth part of his funds for the benefit of the Hospital, burdened with an annuity which continues to be paid to the present day.

The other sum to which reference has been made was a legacy received some years ago from Jamaica; and though the connexion of the party who bestowed it with the Hospital has not been traced as that of Mr. Douglas was, yet the circumstances relating to it are not a little remarkable.

At some period between the years 1770 and 1780, a person of the name of William Ross, was a clerk in the employment of Mr. Home Rigg of Morton, writer to the signet ; and, at the same time, a young woman, of the name of Margaret Murray, was an inmate of his family, where she had been received at an early age; and Mrs. Rigg having had her instructed in millinery and dress-making, she became her personal attendant and waiting-maid. An attachment was formed between these parties, and, to use the expression employed in the letter from Jamaica announcing the legacy, before either of them were " out of their teens," they married. They had only one child, a daughter, Jessie Ross.

The husband was too young and too poor to keep house long, and Mr. Rigg sent him to Jamaica, with a recommendation to a Dr. Gordon, who employed him as a clerk, and with whom he remained for several years. Dr. Gordon died, and Mr. Ross afterwards began business as a merchant in Port Maria, and sent for his wife and daughter, who joined him there. After some time, however, in consequence of unfortunate speculations, he became insolvent. But his daughter, by her talents and industry as a dress-maker, not only supported her parents, but in the course of time realised a very considerable fortune; and shortly before her death, which took place before that of either her father or mother, she executed a will, leaving her whole property to them. The deed having, however, been hurriedly and inartificially drawn, some difficulty arose in ascertaining the proper construction of it ; and the Attorney-General of Jamaica having been consulted on the subject, gave it as his opinion that the will conveyed to Mrs Ross a liferent unaffected by her husband's debts, and a liferent to him if he should survive his wife—the fee simple belonging to Mrs. Ross.

Mr. Ross died in 1802, and in the following year his widow executed a settlement, by which she left the whole of the property to the Orphan Hospital, the value of which, after her death in 1806, was gradually realised and remitted, the last sum being received in the year 1828, and the whole amounting to £7452 : 12 : 3d.

The only reason that was ever stated for this destination may be given in the words of the gentleman who acted as executor and transmitted the legacy. " Mrs. Ross told me," he says, " that her daughter, on the day before she died, " verbally laid this injunction upon her, that, if she outlived " Mr. Ross, she should, as soon as convenient after his death, " make a will, and leave her whole property to the Orphan " Hospital. So that, in reality," he adds, " the Hospital is " indebted to Miss Ross for the donation."

Were it not for the circumstance last mentioned, and could the appropriation of the property have been viewed solely as the act of Mrs. Ross, it would have been a natural inference that she had in her childhood received some benefit from the Institution, and probably had gone from it to the family of Mr. Rigg, who, as well as his father, it is known, took an interest in the Hospital, and both of whom were Members of the Incorporation. Even supposing this to have been the fact, and that the obligations of her mother to the Institution were highly estimated by the daughter, the injunction given by her may in this way be easily accounted for.

But another hypothesis may be indulged, which is, perhaps, equally probable——that after the father's removal to Jamaica, Mrs. Ross and her daughter came to be in straitened and destitute circumstances, and that Mr. Rigg had induced the Managers of the Hospital, although they could not consistently admit her as an orphan into the house, yet to allow Jessie Ross to receive her education with the children under their care, or in some other way to derive important advantages from the Institution. And this may account for her name never having appeared on the roll of its inmates, whilst the considerable sum left by Mr. Rigg to the Hospital, in 1789, may have had some connection with these circumstances.

After all, it may only have been from the knowledge of the Orphan Hospital which she had obtained through the interest taken in it by Mr. Rigg, or by other means, that Miss Ross was induced to single it out as the object of her beneficence.

It is manifest, however, that some strong sense of its value and usefulness must have taken an early hold of her mind, and kept possession of it till the period of her death.

In 1809 a most unhandsome and unwarrantable attack was made on the Orphan Hospital in an article which appeared in the Scots Magazine, and which professed to give an account of a visit to Edinburgh made by Dr. Frank, a German traveller, in which it was insinuated that, for about twelve years preceding, there had been a great declension in the order and management of the Institution, with a variety of animadversions to its prejudice. While the Managers, who were in regular attendance at the Hospital, and whose names might have been a guarantee for the fidelity with which the duties of their charge would be fulfilled, were conscious of the groundlessness of the assertions contained in this paper, they did not, however, rest contented without taking the necessary steps for counteracting the mischievous effects which they might produce. They accordingly invited the Principal and Professor of Divinity in the University, the Presidents of the Royal Colleges of Physicians and Surgeons, and the Lord Provost of the City, personally to make the most ample and minute investigation into the whole arrangements and conduct of the Institution. This they accordingly did, and by a full Report on the subject, which, together with a statement by the Managers, was afterwards inserted in the same Magazine, they completely put down a calumny which, it was evident, had originated in some very narrow, selfish, and interested views.

The Managers seem, no doubt, to have experienced considerable difficulty in permanently filling up the place that had become vacant by the death of Mr. Peebles. But their anxiety, in regard to the real interests of the Institution, appears from the whole course of their proceedings as detailed in the minutes, never for a moment to have been relaxed, and to have been directed, not only to the condition of the inmates of the house, but to the importance of endeavouring to continue some inspection over them when they had left it, as the eye of a parent still watches over the fortunes and happiness of his offspring, long after they have been removed from beneath his domestic roof.

With this view, in 1808, on the suggestion of Mr. Bonar, they commenced the keeping of a more complete record than had yet been done, of the future progress and history of all the children who had been brought up in the Hospital; and required those who had left it, regularly for a certain number of years to appear before them on the day of the annual sermon, in order that some token of encouragement might be given to such as should produce certificates of good conduct from their employers, and that some final mark of approbation at the close of their apprenticeship, or termination of four years' service, might be bestowed on those who had uniformly obtained a character for diligence, honesty, and sobriety. This plan is still followed; and, though it may, to a certain degree, be liable to the objection of introducing the co-operation of motives which are of an order inferior to those by which good men ought to be governed, yet it has been found to furnish a most agreeable point of occasional re-union among those who had once belonged to the same family, and to have had many salutary effects upon the young persons who were trained in the Institution.

In 1812 a considerable addition was made to the accommodations of the Hospital, by the erection of a separate building, which contained a wash-house and laundry, a large schoolroom, a dwelling-house for the Master of the Institution, and apartments for the sick. Several important advantages were gained by this addition; and, among others, a better opportunity was afforded for training the girls to some of those domestic employments by which they might be prepared for the situation of domestic servants,—an object which the Managers had been anxious to promote, and, in attaining which, they have, on the whole, been very successful.

After this date the girls were retained in the Hospital for a longer time than had previously been the case, and did not leave it until they were, in some degree, qualified for entering into family service. And it is an agreeable reflection, that, for many years, very little difficulty has been experienced in finding them situations, the demand being generally greater than the supply. It has been found more embarrassing by far, especially of late years, to procure suitable situations and employments for the boys. With respect to them, the object of the institution embraced nothing beyond the training them with a view to the ordinary occupations of tradesmen and artizans, or, in conformity with a resolution of the Managers, in 1814, the rearing of some of them for country employments, as gardeners and farm-servants. For following out this last idea, it must be obvious, however, that but little op-

portunity has been hitherto enjoyed; and from the general
increase of the population, the circumstances of the times,
and the change which has, unhappily, been introduced in regard to the condition of apprentices,* those favourable open-
ings which formerly existed have been greatly limited, and it
has been found impossible for the Managers, when parting
with the boys, to see them, in every case, provided with situations in the manner they would desire.

No period, however, during the experience of those who at
present have the direction of the Hospital, and no part of the
records of its former history, have been deficient in satisfactory
evidence of the success with which its ultimate design has been
prosecuted, in the rearing and establishing creditably and use-
fully in the world a great number of children who might otherwise have become the prey of idleness, misery, and vice, and,
as the chief means of securing that end, of early instilling
into their minds the principles of religion. Not a few individuals who have filled, and many who still occupy most respectable stations in society, to which their own good conduct
has advanced them, have not been ashamed to acknowledge
that it was to the formation of their character while in the
Orphan Hospital that all the advantages they have attained
were chiefly to be ascribed. And the letters received occa-
sionally from those who look back with gratitude on their connexion with it; the acknowledgments, made by others in a different form to the same effect; and a variety of facts and anec-
dotes which might here be stated, are so many testimonies
that the Divine blessing has from the very beginning rested
on the undertaking.†

Any particular detail on this subject, however, would here be
unsuitable, and an opportunity will afterwards arise for advert-

* In former times, the general practice in regard to apprentices was,
that where they had no parental roof at hand, they were received into
the families of their masters, and were instructed and watched over,
in all respects, as their own children. Now-a-days, this, with some
other good customs and habits, has greatly disappeared, and, if the sti-
pulated amount of bodily labour be but yielded, the youth, in such circumstances, are left very much to themselves, and to all the buffetings
and temptations of a selfish and ensnaring world.

† A short account of two interesting children who were educated
in the Hospital, was printed by an individual in 1811, as a tract for
the benefit of the children of the Institution, and has lately been re-
printed.

ing to the moral tendency and effects of the Institution. Meanwhile, and without selecting any other prominent events in the course of its history, it will be proper now to notice those circumstances out of which has arisen an important era in regard to the Hospital—its removal from the house which it had so long occupied, and the situation where it had been so well known.

When the ground on which the first Hospital was built was selected and acquired, it possessed many advantages, of which none can form an estimate at the present day without throwing themselves back in imagination to that period in the progress of Edinburgh when the New Town and the North Bridge were as yet uncontemplated,—when the Trinity College Church and a row of small houses leading up by Calton Street to what was then called Multrees Hill, were the only buildings at all contiguous to the ground,—and when the whole space to the west and north was a free and unbroken line of fields, part of them known by the name of Bearsford's Park. In the course of time, however, circumstances changed, and that which had originally been a clear, detached, and airy situation, as the site of every such Institution ought to be, became, comparatively, a close and confined spot, artificially sunk down from its natural level, cut off from every rural appearance and association, and surrounded almost on all sides by lofty buildings, with the drains from the New Town passing under the very walls of the house.

It is curious to review the recorded feelings of the Managers, as circumstances, from time to time, arose, to affect the situation of the Hospital, and the efforts by which they endeavoured to ward off or counteract the inroads that were made on its comfort.

In 1768 they made a vigorous but unsuccessful attempt to prevent the erection of the Theatre on a part of Forglen's Park, contiguous to the Hospital, which had been obtained for that purpose, and which they considered would, both physically and morally, be most injurious to the Institution. Two years afterwards, they rejected an application which was made for opening a road to the Theatre at the west end of the Hospital, although for their acquiescence in this they were offered the proceeds of an annual performance for the Institution. In 1774, when the drain for the Register House was constructed, every precaution at the time thought necessary was adopted to prevent its being prejudicial to the Hospital. The same year, after the prevalence of a contagious fever, by which forty-two out of fifty-four inmates of the house were affected, the greatest pains were taken to improve its ventilation, and to remove every nuisance from the neighbourhood. In 1779, the Managers hired a house at Leith, to which the children of feeble constitutions were removed for the advantage of the better air which they there enjoyed. In 1780, the strongest opposition was given, but in vain, to the erection of the slaughter-house on a part of the old Physic Gardens, the filth and corruption arising from which would, in the opinion of several eminent physicians who had been consulted, prove hurtful to the health of the children. In 1782, in order to prevent the multiplication of such evils, and to remove those that then existed, they applied for and obtained a long lease of that part of the Physic Gardens which was directly in front of the Hospital's ground, and which had come to be occupied by the boilers of tar and oil, and others who carried on similar disagreeable operations. In 1796, a special meeting was held, for taking measures to resist the erection of a farrier's forge under one of the arches of the North Bridge, and immediately to the west of the Hospital, which threatened to be both dangerous and offensive. In 1811, when the new North Bridge buildings were contemplated, the Managers expressed the strong sense which they felt as to the injury that would arise from them to the Institution, and even hesitated for a while in carrying forward the additional erections which they had projected on their own ground, from the idea that an entire removal might be rendered necessary. In 1817, they declined considering a favourable proposal that was made to them, for feuing a part of their ground for a range of buildings on the east, similar to those that had been constructed on the west side of the Bridge; and in 1822, another advantageous offer was in like manner declined for allotting a portion of their ground for erecting a military barrack, and expressly with the view of preserving, in as far as they could, the airiness of the situation.

In the midst of all this, and to bear the Institution up as they best could against the tide that had on all hands set in so unfavourably for the position of the Hospital, and which, notwithstanding all that they had succeeded in preventing, had materially encroached on the advantages which it once possessed, the Managers introduced such changes in the internal arrangements of the house, and in regard to the food and clothing of the children, as they thought most conducive to the preservation of their health; and they also made arrangements for their enjoying regular seabathing and more frequent excursions into the country than they had been previously allowed, besides introducing those gymnastic exercises, which, within certain limits, tend so greatly in young persons to animate the spirits and to invigorate the bodily frame.

But, notwithstanding these efforts and precautions, circumstances soon arose which awakened the most intense and painful anxiety in the minds of the Managers. In 1823, a Memorial was presented to them on the subject of the health of the children by the late Mr. Bryce, the Medical Officer of the Hospital, and Dr. Abercrombie, who, from the time of his becoming a Member of the Incorporation, had taken the warmest interest in the welfare of the children,—in which such views were presented as led to the first serious impression of the necessity of a removal of the Hospital. From the formidable nature of such a step, however, and the encroachment which it would inevitably make upon the funds, the idea was at first entertained only in conjunction with that of the Managers being enabled to make an advantageous sale of the house and ground then occupied by the Hospital; and a variety of schemes were brought forward with a view to this object, while every thing was in the mean time done which the Medical Gentlemen could devise and recommend, in order to counteract the evil that had arisen.

Early in 1828, however, the attention of the Managers was anew awakened and arrested by the appalling fact, that within the space of eleven months there had occurred no fewer than ten deaths among the children; and by a fresh representation on the subject from Dr. Abercrombie and Mr. Brown, then and still the faithful and assiduous Surgeon to the Hospital, who reiterated the former statements,—that whilst the age between seven and fourteen years was universally the most healthy period of human life, and all the calculations that had been made of the probabilities of life during that period, gave a general annual average of deaths as one in one hundred and twenty-three persons,—and whilst the returns from other Institutions, where children were maintained in circumstances similar to those of the Orphans exhibited an average of deaths as one in one hundred and twelve individuals, the proportion that had been found for some time to exist in the Hospital was one in twenty-three! After making every allowance for the predisposition to disease which, from obvious causes, might be supposed to attach to the children of the Hospital, and for every circumstance by which their health might be supposed to be affected, the whole of the Medical Gentlemen who were consulted concurred in giving it as their opinion, that the situation of the house had become so unfavourable, that to this, as the chief cause, could be ascribed the high degree of mortality which prevailed, and they stated that they could suggest no other remedy than an entire removal of the Hospital to a different situation.

This opinion was decisive, and paramount as to the duty of the Managers. The question came at once to be, whether it was preferable to maintain the usual number of admissions, and to remain in the old house with the prospect of the continuance of such a mortality,—or to provide a new one, and to take fewer children, with the prospect of health : and here there could be no room for a moment's hesitation. The Managers, therefore, and the Members of the Incorporation, to whom the whole matters were regularly submitted, immediately resolved upon a removal,—their sense of duty prevailed over every fear as to the deficiency of means, and they trusted, that by the sale of their old house and ground, the lapsing of certain annuities, and the increased liberality of benevolent individuals, they might be enabled, in the course of time, to repair the reduction in the number of the children to be admitted, which, in the mean while, was unavoidable. They, accordingly, feued a piece of ground at Dean, and proceeded to the erection of the new Hospital, to which the Institution has just been removed.

In selecting this spot, the Managers were influenced by the elevated nature of the situation, and by its convenient proximity to the City, while it was yet at such a distance from it, and so circumstanced, as to exclude any apprehension of the recurrence of the evil that had been experienced in the former house, especially as a very considerable space of ground had prudently been secured.

The next object of the Managers was to obtain a suitable plan for the building, and for this purpose they employed Mr. Thomas Hamilton, an architect of great skill and repu-

D

tation. The internal accommodation and conveniences, being of primary importance, were first considered ; and the Managers think that in this respect the new Hospital will be found eminently adapted for its purpose. A plan of the mode in which the different floors are laid out is subjoined in the Appendix, No. 8, and will better explain the different arrangements than any description can do. It may only be necessary here to direct attention to the judicious separation of the apartments assigned to the boys and girls, and to the accommodations for the sick, which, though under the same roof, are entirely detached from the other parts of the house, are secluded from noise by the intervention of double doors, thick walls, and distinct passages, and at the same time are so disposed as not to interrupt a free communication among the surrounding apartments. A stove chamber is placed in the vault below the entrance hall, and has been fitted up upon the most approved principles, so as, without superseding the use of fires in certain of the rooms, to diffuse the necessary warmth throughout the upper parts of the house in winter, while in summer it may be used for cooling them. Water has also been plentifully introduced into all the apartments where it may be required, and almost every room is supplied with gas.

With regard to the exterior design, the Managers were placed in a situation of some difficulty. On the one hand they had to study economy; on the other, nobody would have justified them in putting down in the commanding situation which they had obtained, a building at all resembling an ordinary workhouse or penitentiary, or any thing even that was mean in its appearance, or out of keeping with its proximity to the metropolis and with the surrounding objects, or in violation of the improved taste of the times. They did not however feel warranted in incurring the expense inseparable from a building in the pure Grecian or Roman character, or even in the less imposing, though scarcely less expensive, style of the Gothic or Elisabethan architecture. They endeavoured to adopt a middle course; yet to have everything done in the most solid and substantial manner, which they were confident would in the end be found to be the truest economy. The general effect which has been given by the nature of the site to the appearance of the building may lead to the impression with some persons, that it is too showy and ambitious. But, the leading ornamental features, such as the terrace and the towers, are adjuncts of essential utility, and any minor decorations have been introduced at a very trifling expense. Besides, without some degree of ornament at least, no building perhaps can present that cheerfulness of aspect which may be said to exercise a certain moral influence, and which tends to impart to the individuals that inhabit it, especially to the young, a corresponding cheerfulness of mind and a variety of lively associations.

The original contract for the building amounted to £11,849. The inclosing walls and drains, the laying out of the ground, the introduction of water, gas, and heated air, and other necessary things, will no doubt make a considerable addition to this sum, but the whole has been accomplished at as moderate an expense as could reasonably be expected, and, what in such a case is a most important object, the house has been rendered complete at once, and will be found capable of accommodating two hundred children, when circumstances require and the funds will admit of the number being increased to that extent. In the mean time, it is obvious that the absorption of capital rendered indispensable by the erection of the new house must, for a while, circumscribe the number of admissions, but it ought also to stimulate to fresh exertions for increasing the disposable funds of the Institution.

The details which have thus been given may be sufficient for exhibiting a view of the past history and progress, and of the present circumstances of the Orphan Hospital. And a few additional observations appear all that is necessary to complete the objects proposed by this publication.

1st, In regard to the original principle and inherent tendency of such an Institution.

It is neither to be denied nor disguised, that, among the multitude of charitable establishments which exist in this country, there may be some, which, originating in a very sincere but short-sighted philanthropy, do actually not conduce to the real and permanent interests of society; by which, especially in certain instances, some of the very evils may be multiplied which they were instituted to remedy, and of which the strong description that has been given may be

but too true, " that they are little better than a tax upon industry for the support of idleness."

With such institutions, however, an establishment like the
Orphan Hospital is neither to be confounded nor compared ;
provided always, that the original object be steadily kept in
view, and that it be fenced and protected by the most rigid
attention to the nature of every claim which is made upon its
funds. The circumstances of misfortune and distress which
it professes to meet are such as are involuntary, inevitable,
and irremediable by other means. This statement, no doubt,
assumes that the persons admitted to the benefits of the Institution are those, who, by any of the sudden and over-
whelming visitations of Providence to which mankind are
liable, have in early life been deprived of their parents, and
precipitated into a state of entire helplessness and destitution,
without a relation that possesses the means, or an individual
on whom the obligation lies, of becoming their guardians and
protectors, and of supplying to them the place of parents ;
and for whose support and education no other provision of
any kind whatsoever exists, or can be called into operation.
*And this is the real, the only class for whom the Orphan Hos-
pital is designed.* Whilst no man in possession of his senses
will voluntarily make his children orphans—while every sane
man, on the contrary, will strive to ward off that event by
which they would become so, it is evident that there exists
in nature itself a certain safeguard against the extension of the
evils for which such an Institution is intended to provide a remedy, and against the spontaneous establishment of a claim to
a participation in its benefits. As in the case of life insurance,
where a posthumous advantage is secured by an annual payment, a man, from the mere love of life, and the principle of
self-preservation, would wish to make the worst pecuniary
bargain that is possible ; so, in general, will every human
being struggle to keep his children, by the interval of as
great a distance as he can, from coming within the range of
the benefits of an Orphan Hospital.

Yet it may be said of this, and similar institutions, that,
whilst no one would deliberately desire that his offspring
should ever become the recipients of their bounty, or by any
distinct deed actually invest them with the character of those
for whose relief they are established, there may nevertheless
spring up, among the unseen and almost insensible processes

of low and vitiated minds, such a dependence upon some future contingent provision for their families, as to render them more improvident in their habits than they otherwise would be, and indifferent to the employment of means for securing the comfort of their families. Now, it is no doubt true that a very pernicious course of reasoning such as this may take place in some minds. But, in the first place, when it does happen, it is not in cases where their own death is the condition to be interposed, but where some provision is attainable for their children while they themselves are alive, by means of which their present labour may be relaxed, and their present indulgences enlarged ; and, in the second place, this immoral habit of thinking will be found to exist chiefly, or almost entirely, in one of two cases—either where *a right* is possessed, or can be established, to the contemplated advantage or relief, or where the sphere of the charitable provision is so vague, miscellaneous, and indefinite, or where it is so interestedly or indiscriminately administered, as to form something like a foundation, if not for a sure participation in it, yet for such a degree of hope or expectation as is sufficient for the purpose.

But if there is nothing in its moral tendency necessarily injurious, it may be stated, 2*dly*, That the institutes and practice of the Orphan Hospital, and especially the mode followed in the selection of the cases for admission, are as carefully adapted as possible for the attainment of its original design, and for counteracting all abuse.

The precise objects for whom it is intended have already been defined. It is not an Institution for the children of those who have possessed any certain *status*, or acquired any privileges in connection with some corporation or particular branch of the community, in virtue of which alone an admission to its benefits may be secured. Neither are the admissions determined by the votes of a large body of subscribers, as is the case in some other Institutions having a similar object, where the annual revenue arises chiefly from those contributions by which a right of voting may be purchased, and the effect of which, there is reason to fear, may be, that a constant competition is kept up for obtaining the interest of individuals, and the least friendless class of objects is the most likely to be preferred. In the case of the Orphan Hospital, the circumstances of the severest destitution form the only preferable claim to its benefits. There is a limit as to age, and a restriction in

one or two other points which are indispensable; but in selecting the cases every one is tried by its own merits, and by
a laborious comparison with the circumstances of others; and
at no period has any thing like interest or favour been allowed
to prevail. The particulars required to be stated in the petitions
are ample and minute, and are framed with a view to elicit
the real facts of every case,—these must be most amply veri-
fied and attested;—an abstract of all the petitions is prepared,
and remains for the consideration of the Managers for some
time previous to the selection, in order that they may prose-
cute their enquiries deliberately, and fully weigh the different
claims,—a rigid scrutiny by personal inspection of the children, and an examination of their relations or friends has also
been established, and securities adopted not only against
fraud and deception, but against the admission of those who
have any adequate resources, or whose natural guardians
would seek to remove to the shoulders of a public institution
a burden which Providence has placed upon their own.
Every thing, in short, has been done that could be devised
for insuring the right application of the funds, and for cutting
off the occasion of injurious expectations on the part of any.

3dly, The extent of real and solid good which has been,
and which may be accomplished by the Orphan Hospital, is a
subject of very interesting reflection.

One primary advantage of such an Institution is, that it
has to do with the young, and in this respect it occupies one
of the most hopeful of all the provinces of charity—rescuing
from a multitude of moral and physical evils those in the beginning of their days, who, in all human probability, would
have been drifted or driven away into the very abyss of de-
struction, and furnishing them not only with the means of life,
but teaching them the way of living for the great ends of life.
The most ordinary humanity prompts to the relief of tempo-
rary wants,—*that* is the most valuable kind of charity which
labours to prevent misery, by the prevention of ignorance
and vice,—*that* the highest species of benevolence, which
seeks to render the unfortunate and the destitute permanently
happy, by training them to the right exercise of their own
faculties, by practically convincing them of the value of a
habit of virtuous industry, and imparting to them just senti-
ments as to the ends and intention of their being. Besides,
and above all, in the daily endeavour to imbue the young

mind with the principles and precepts of the Bible, there is to be found the only efficacious antidote to the snares of the world, and the only solid foundation for a substantially good character. These, once infused, circulate silently and imperceptibly, like the blood in the human body, and, nourished by the growing observation and experience of minds early tutored to reflection, become the elements of all that is estimable, and the spring of all that is truly happy in human life. It were wrong—very wrong—to confine the efficacy of religious instruction to mere mechanical effects, or to suppose that real excellence of character is the necessary consequence even of the best tuition and discipline. Still, it is true, that according to their youthful training men generally live—that as they live so they commonly die,—and that early sobriety, early knowledge of religion, and early habits of self-denial, are the surest pathway to honour and felicity.

Let any considerate man reflect but for a moment on the multitude of children, who, by the negligence and immorality of their parents, have been left entirely to themselves, or almost necessarily abandoned to profligacy and vice, and who, by the force of early training and example, as the means, might have been saved from the gulf that has long ago devoured them—and will he not find it a very rousing and quickening thought? The right remedy for this evil, could it be attained, would be found in the full and universal discharge of the parental duties, and the Orphan Hospital can do nothing to relax these obligations. But it strives to save those who have none to save or to care for them. Had any great proportion of those, who, by neglect in their young days, have been wrecked and cast away, been saved by the promised blessing of God on the watchful care of those to whom they were committed as a sacred and solemn trust, from the courses that have ruined them, the state of society might have been very different from what it is felt to be at the present day, and the jail and the gibbet have been spared many of their victims. And, even bad as the moral condition of the lower orders, in many respects, indubitably is, can any one say that it might not have been worse but for the intervention of the means by which many have been preserved? No one can see or calculate the amount of evil which has been prevented, and of the thousands who have been reared in the Orphan Hospital to knowledge, industry, and virtue, and have had the fair opportunity afforded them of living well, and of dying well, and have done both, how many, may it be supposed, would have fallen a prey to crime and to irremediable sorrow, had they not been snatched as brands from the very burning! There is an intense interest superadded to these reflections, when we think of the contagious and descending nature of vice, which propagates itself, and may widen the tide of human misery to a thousand generations. It is consolatory to reflect, on the other hand, that there is a similar, if not an equally powerful tendency in what is good, and that, by the instrumentality of such an institution as the Orphan Hospital, many have been brought forward into life, to occupy its stations and to discharge its duties with credit and advantage, to shed the blessings of religion and of moral health throughout the circle in which they moved, and to train up a new generation in their turn to inherit and to perpetuate their character and their principles.

4th, The style of education and the course of training followed in the Hospital are quite plain and unpretending. Nothing more is aimed at than the preparation of the children for the ordinary situations of life. Reading and spelling, writing, arithmetic, and geography, are the only branches in which the whole of them are instructed, whilst every method is pursued for exercising and expanding their minds consistently with the place which they are to occupy in the world; and the girls, as already noticed, are taught those arts which may qualify them for their appropriate spheres.

Their food and clothing are also plain, but substantial; and, in regard to these, various improvements have from time to time been introduced, in as far as they tended to promote the health and comfort of the children, and were compatible with the strictest economy. This, indeed, the Managers have sought uniformly to study: and, in proof of it, it may be sufficient to mention that, including the whole salaries and fees of the establishment—the expense of maintenance and clothing—of books, furniture, and utensils—of buildings and repairs on the house—of coals, candles, soap, and all incidental expenses, the average cost for each member of the family has for several years been between £13 and £14 annually.

5th, The Orphan Hospital, let it not be forgotten, is a Na-

tional and not a local institution. Some parts of its history
that have been alluded to may have indicated this ; but, in
farther illustration of it, it may be stated, that, without any
previous knowledge, and far less without any premeditated
intention, the children who were admitted at Whitsunday last
were found, after their election, to have had the places of their
nativity or residence as follows :—

Arbroath,	-	One.	Edinburgh, - - -	Three.
Auchtergaven,		One.	Glasgow, - - -	One.
Dalkeith,	- -	One.	Leith, - - - -	One.
Dumfries,	- -	One.	Perth, - - - -	One.
Dunse,	- - -	One.	Queensferry, - -	One.

6th, The Orphan Hospital is a Corporation, but it is not
what is understood by the title of a close Corporation. There
is a change annually made in the individuals to whom
the management of it is confided, and besides those who
in virtue of their office belong to it, every individual who is
a donor is admissible, and is actually admitted, as a Member
of the Incorporation. Quarterly meetings are regularly sum-
moned of the whole Members, at which the proceedings of
the Managers are detailed—the accounts of the Institution are
open to every individual of the body, and the control of
its affairs is entirely in their hands. It may be mentioned,
however, and mentioned as one chief cause probably of the
satisfaction and success with which it has all along been con-
ducted, that at no period has the spirit of feud, dissension,
or party, had any place in the management of the Charity,
but seems to have been uniformly scared away from it, and
a feeling of cordiality and friendship to have cemented those
together, who at any time have been associated in the administration of its affairs.

Finally, An appeal is here made in behalf of the Institution to all who can assist by their countenance and co-operation
in promoting its objects or its success,—more especially to
those who may have it in their power to direct to a channel of
so much real usefulness, any of those sums which are destin-
ed to purposes of philanthropy and benevolence, and which
can be so appropriated in perfect consistency with every other
just claim or obligation.

As there is something very striking to an attentive reader
of the Scriptures in the peculiar manner in which the orphan
and the fatherless are spoken of and referred to,—in the early

E

and repeated precepts given to Israel, for their special safety and protection—in the solemn warnings delivered by the Prophets against indifference, neglect, or injustice towards them—in the judgments by which these precepts were expressly vindicated, and these threatenings fulfilled,—something most impressive in the examples which are furnished by the inspired history of those who, deprived in their infancy of a father's and a mother's care, were nevertheless raised to stations of the greatest honour and usefulness, as if they belonged to a class that was the peculiar charge of a watchful and kind Providence,—something, above all, emphatic in the title and prerogative which the Almighty has himself claimed of being " the Father of the fatherless in his holy habita-" tion,"—so to the man of religious principle and feeling, as well as to every friend to the happiness of his race, this cannot be a fruitless appeal in behalf of an Institution that has been fostered by the liberality and upheld by the Christian zeal of so many in former times, and which must still depend for its efficacy and success upon the same virtues in those of the present and of future generations.

FORM OF A BEQUEST TO THE HOSPITAL.

I give and bequeath to the Incorporation of the Orphan Hospital of Edinburgh, the sum of £   , to be applied to its support and maintenance, agreeably to the Rules of the Institution.

APPENDIX.

No. I.

LETTERS PATENT IN FAVOUR OF THE ORPHAN HOSPITAL.

GEORGE R.

OUR SOVEREIGN LORD, CONSIDERING That an humble petition hath been presented to his Majesty by Thomas Dundas of Fingask, merchant and late Baillie of Edinburgh, Preses, and in name of a general meeting of the contributors towards erecting an Orphan Hospital and Work-house in Edinburgh, SETTING FORTH That, notwithstanding the many excellent laws made in that part of his Majesty's kingdom called *Scotland,* for the education and entertainment, and setting to work the poor thereof; great numbers of children, orphans, or whose parents cannot bear the charges of their education and maintenance, are abandoned to ignorance, idleness and vice, and so become a great burden when young, and a much heavier when old, upon society; *and that* they, taking this into consideration, had, for remedying of the said evils, *agreed* to give and mortify certain sums of money, to be applied for defraying the charge of maintaining the said destitute children, and instructing them in reading, writing, and arithmetic, in the principles of our most holy religion, and in such trades, labour, handicraft, and offices, as, upon proper trial and examination, shall be found best adapted to their several geniuses and capacities; *and that* the design was approven of by several persons of distinction, as well Nobility as others, and by the Lords of Session, the Magistrates and Town Council of the City of Edinburgh, the Faculty of Advocates, the Society of Clerks to the Signet, and many other charitable persons, as also by several Synods and Presbyteries of the Church of Scotland; *and that* the said contributors had, in several general meetings, considered of, and agreed to certain rules for the better management of the said Orphan Hospital and Workhouse. AND HIS MAJESTY UNDERSTANDING that the said contributors have already made a considerable progress towards the erecting and establishing of the said Orphan Hospital and Workhouse, and judging that the foresaid design, if rightly managed, may prove a great benefit, not only to the poor, but likewise to the nation in general, and tend much to the encouragement of piety, charity, and industry, DOES THEREFORE AP-POINT a Patent to be past and expede under the seal appointed by the Articles of Union to be kept and used in Scotland, in place of the great seal thereof, *constituting, erecting,* and *incorporating,* as his Majesty, for himself and his Royal Successors, by these presents, *constitutes, erects, incorporates,* and perpetually *establishes* and *confirms* his Majesty's trusty and well-beloved the Lord Justice-General for Scotland, &c. (see page 46 of this Appendix,) *and such* other persons as shall be elected, in manner after directed, *into* one body politic and corporate, or legal incorporation and society in deed and name, under the name and title of THE ORPHAN HOSPITAL AND WORKHOUSE AT EDINBURGH; and as such corporation, and by such name, to have a perpetual succession.   AND HIS MAJESTY WILLS, GRANTS, AND DECLARES, That the said Corporation and their successors foresaid, by the name foresaid, shall have full power, and be able and capable in law, to purchase, take, hold, and enjoy in fee, heritably and irredeemably, for the use and behoof of the said Corporation, any lands, tenements, houses, annuities, jurisdictions, and other heritages, not exceeding, in the whole, the clear yearly rent of *one thousand pounds sterling,* after deduction of feu-duties or chief rent, cesses, ministers' or schoolmasters' stipends and fees, and other public burdens; *and for that end,* to take, receive, and enjoy, for the behoof foresaid, *all* and whatever mortifications and donations of heritages, goods, money, and other estates and effects real and personal, which are already or shall hereafter be made, given, or granted in favour of the said corporation : *and to employ* and bestow such heritages, goods, money, estates, and effects real and personal, so purchased, gifted, and mortified, and produce and proceeds thereof, for, and towards the maintenance and instruction of children in the Hospital and Workhouse of the said Corporation, and government and service thereof, and of the said children, in such manner as the said Corporation and their successors, or major part of such of them as shall convene at their general meetings herein after directed, shall think reasonable and proper; *and also* to sell and dispose of such lands and other heritages purchased and acquired, or to be purchased and acquired by the said Corporation and their successors, as they, or major part of them as shall convene at their general meetings herein after directed, shall judge profitable and convenient for the said Corporation.   PROVIDED ALWAYS, That such sale and disposal of any part of their heritages be made with the consent and approbation of his Majesty's trusty and well-beloved the Lord Justice-General, the Lord President of the Court of Session, the Lord Chief Baron of the Court of Exchequer, the Lord Justice-Clerk, his Majesty's Advocate, and his Majesty's Solicitor for Scotland, the Lord Provost of Edinburgh, and the Keeper of his Majesty's Signet in Scotland, all of them for the time being, or any three of them : *And that* the said Corporation, and their successors by name foresaid, may and shall sue and be sued, plead and defend in all actions and processes whatever, civil or criminal, and act and do all and every other lawful matter and thing, in as ample manner and form as any other body politic or corporate, or any other his Majesty's subjects, but with and under the provisions before written, and may have a common seal for the public business of the said Corporation, and break, make new, and alter the same at pleasure: AND that the said Corporation and their successors shall and may make, constitute, and ordain, and again repeal or alter, such and so many bye-laws, constitutions, rules, and or-dinances, as they, or major part of such of them as shall convene at any of their general meetings herein after directed, shall judge necessary and convenient for the well ordering and governing of the said Corpora-tion, and the officers thereof, and children to be maintained and in-structed in the Hospital and Workhouse of the same; and with and under such mulcts and penalties upon the transgressors or disobeyers as they shall think reasonable: *Provided always*, That such bye-laws and rules be not contrary to the true intent and meaning of these pre-sents, or repugnant to the laws and statutes of the kingdom. AND, for the better execution of the purposes aforesaid, his Majesty hereby *gives* and *grants* to the said Corporation, and their successors, full power and authority, that they, and their successors for ever, may meet and con-vene four times in the year, or oftner, at such times and places as they shall think fit, for the better management of the estate and affairs of the said Corporation, these times and places being always settled and de-termined by the bye-laws thereof; and at such meetings, the said Cor-poration and their successors, or major part of them, who shall convene thereat, shall and may choose and elect such person or persons to be mem-bers of the said Corporation, besides these herein appointed, as they or said major part shall think beneficial to the same, such persons to be elect-ed being always contributors or donors of some money less or more for the use and benefit of the said Corporation; and shall and may choose and elect yearly, out of the members of the said Corporation for the time being, fifteen persons to be managers of the said Corporation; and shall and may elect and choose any person or persons to be treasurers, clerks, ac-countants, comptrollers, masters, and such other officers or servants one or more, as shall be thought necessary for the said Corporation or children, and with such salaries, fees, and allowances as the said Cor-poration shall think reasonable: *Provided always*, That none of the managers shall be capable to be elected a treasurer, or into any other office dependent upon the Corporation, during the time of his being a manager; and which managers shall continue in that office for no longer space than one year, unless re-chosen, and until the first general meet-ing thereafter; and, in case of the death or incapacity of any one of them, his room and place shall be filled up by another member to be chosen by the next general meeting thereafter, and to continue till the next general election; but the said treasurer and other officers may con-tinue in their respective offices for such space of time as by the bye-laws of the said Corporation from time to time shall be appointed: AND that the said fifteen managers, or any five of them, shall have the manage-ment, direction, and government of all and sundry the estates and effects real and personal, and other interest and concerns, affairs and business of the said corporation, and of the officers thereof, and children instructed and maintained thereby, and may meet when and where they please for that purpose; but shall act and manage according to the bye-laws and ordinances of the said Corporation, so far as shall be therein directed. And HIS MAJESTY ordains the said Letters Patent to be past under the foresaid seal appointed in place of the great seal of Scotland, *per saltum*, and without passing any other seal; and for which these presents shall be to the Lord Keeper of the said seal, and to the director of his Majesty's Chancery a sufficient warrant. GIVEN at his Majesty's Court at Kensington, the twenty-fifth day of June one thousand seven hundred and forty-two, in the sixteenth year of his Majesty's reign.

TWEEDDALE.

This Patent passed the seals the 6th and 12th days of August 1742.

No. II.

STATUTES OR BYE-LAWS

OF THE

ORPHAN HOSPITAL AT EDINBURGH.

1. *General Meeting.*

THAT there shall be four General Meetings of the Corporation in each year, viz. on the second Monday of February, June, August, and November, respectively, at twelve o'clock noon, in the Hospital, or any other place previously appointed by the Corporation, with the power of adjournment as they shall see cause : Provided always, That, upon any emergency, the President of the Corporation of former meeting, the Treasurer, or any three of the Managers hereafter mentioned, may call a General Meeting on three days' notice, given in the Edinburgh Evening Courant and Caledonian Mercury.

II. *Election of Officers.*

That the General Meeting in August each year shall elect a President, Treasurer, Accountant, Comptroller, and Clerk; all of whom are to continue for one year only, unless they shall be re-elected : That the said Meeting shall also elect fifteen Governors or Managers; of whom three shall go off each year, according to seniority : That all of these persons, except the Clerk, shall serve *gratis*.

III. *Committee of Managers.*

That the Committee of Managers shall have the oversight and direc-

tion of the whole business of the Corporation, and shall do therein
agreeably to statutes and bye-laws which are hereby established, or
shall from time to time be adopted by the said Corporation : That they
shall meet statedly on the first Friday of every month, at twelve o'clock,
or at such other hour as they shall from time to time appoint, within
the Hospital-house, or any other more convenient place in Edinburgh,
with power of adjournment, as they shall see cause ; and, upon any
emergency, the President of the Corporation, or of the Committee, the
Treasurer, or any two of the Managers, may call a meeting, by ordering billets to be issued, warning the Managers to meet at a proper time
and place : That five shall be a quorum : That, for the better despatch
of their business, the Managers shall divide themselves into four Sub-
Committees, viz. one for managing the matters of law, another for au-
diting the accounts, a third for superintending the internal economy of
the house, and a fourth for superintending the education of the children : That the Managers shall keep a regular journal or record of all
their proceedings, and report the same to the quarterly meetings of the
Corporation.

IV.—Capital Stock.

That in all time coming, the Corporation, and the Managers, shall be
careful not to diminish their capital stock, by expending more than the
annual revenue, or otherwise, except in case of extreme necessity ; in
which case, a meeting of the Corporation, consisting of at least fifteen
Members, of whom at least five must be Managers, shall deliberately
consider the matter, and refer the determination of the same to a subsequent meeting, of which the quorum must be the same ; and that
this meeting shall and may authorise the applying part of the stock to
the relief of the then necessity : Provided always, That the meeting
which authorises such application, shall resolve and enact, that such
diminution shall be replaced to the capital stock out of the annual revenue, as expeditiously as the then circumstances and annual expenses
of the Hospital will permit.

V. Purchase of Land.

That when it shall be thought proper to employ any of the funds of
the Corporation in the purchase of lands or houses, the Managers shall
ask the advice of the General Meeting thereupon, and act accordingly.

VI. Lending Money.

That the Managers shall lend no part of the stock of the Corporation
on heritable security, without a written Report from the Law-Commit-
tee that they are satisfied with the security offered ; which Report
shall be engrossed in the minutes of the Managers ; and that they
shall lend no part of their stock on personal security, without having at
least two persons, reputed sufficient, bound conjunctly and severally for
the same : That when any proposal is made to the Managers for bor-
rowing any part of the said stock, the same shall be referred to a subsequent meeting of the said Managers, to be held at the interval of at

least twenty-four hours; of which meeting all the Managers are to be duly advertised, and at least seven must be present.

VII. *Borrowing Money.*

That none of the Managers, officers, or servants of the Corporation, shall borrow, or be received as obligants, co-obligants, or cautioners for any part of the funds or stock of the Hospital.

VIII. *Duty of the Treasurer.*

That the Treasurer shall have power to receive all donations, collections, and legacies, and, in general, to manage the whole revenue and stock of the Hospital, subject to the direction of the Corporation and the Managers; and that he shall find security for his intromissions with the same: That he shall make out his accounts quarterly, viz. on the 1st day of February, May, August, and November, respectively: That the same shall be laid before and audited by the Sub-Committee of Accounts, and shall, by them, be reported to the next Ordinary Meeting of the Managers: That he shall annually exhibit to the Managers a general abstract of the stock, revenue, and expense of the Hospital for the preceding year; which shall be reported by the said Managers to the Meeting of the Corporation to be held on the second Monday of August in each year; in order that the said Meeting, if they approve his accounts, may discharge him of his intromissions: That he may be present in all the Meetings of the Managers, and have an equal voice with them in all matters under their administration, excepting only what may concern his own accounts.

IX. *Duty of Accountant.*

That the Accountant shall examine all the Treasurer's accounts and vouchers, and all other accounts relating to the stock and revenue of the Hospital, and transmit the same with his opinion to the Comptroller: That he shall direct the framing and keeping all the books and accounts of the stock, revenue, expense, and disbursements of the Hospital.

X. *Duty of Comptroller.*

That the Comptroller shall likewise examine all the Treasurer's accounts and vouchers, together with all the other accounts which concern the Hospital or Corporation, and give his opinion thereon to the Managers: That he and the Accountant may be present in all the meetings of the Managers, and have an equal voice with them in all matters which may come before them.

XI. *Duty of Clerk.*

That the Clerk shall attend all the meetings of the Corporation and the Managers, and shall write and register all their proceedings: That he shall copy and keep all the accounts and books which concern the affairs, funds, and disbursements of the Hospital, as they shall be made up by the Treasurer, Accountant and Comptroller, and agreeably to the directions of the Managers; and that he shall have such yearly salary as the Corporation, upon report of the Managers, shall appoint.

XII. *Duty of Teacher.*

That the Master or Teacher of the Hospital shall be chosen annually; and that he shall be of good reputation, exemplary for piety, gravity, temper, and prudence, and well experienced in teaching: That he shall have the inspection of the morals and conduct of the whole children, as well without as within the school; and shall admonish, reprove, and correct them for their faults: That he shall take care that every one in the family shall rise at six in the morning from 1st March to 1st October, and go to bed at ten at night; and that from 1st October to 1st March, they shall rise at seven in the morning, and go to bed at nine at night; and that they assemble every morning and evening for the worship of God, by prayer, reading the Scriptures, and singing psalms: That he shall instruct all in the house in the principles of the Christian reformed religion, and take care that they worship God in secret, as well as with the family: That upon each Lord's Day, all in the Hospital shall go regularly to Church, and there join in public worship; and, in the evening, the master shall call them together, catechise them from the larger or shorter catechism, and read religious books with them: That he shall allow none of the children to go out of the Hospital on the Lord's Day, except on some necessary occasion, and leave given: That he shall attend in the school, and teach the children reading, writing, arithmetic, and church music, at such hours as shall be appointed: That he shall be careful to have the boys employed in such work as shall be from time to time directed by the managers: That he shall receive regulations for his conduct from the Managers; who, upon any failure or neglect, may admonish him, and, if they see cause, may suspend him from his office: and, That he shall have such yearly salary as shall be deemed proper by the Corporation or Managers.

XIII. *Duty of Housekeeper.*

That the Mistress or Housekeeper shall be chosen annually, and shall be free from the burden of children, of unblemished character for virtue and piety, and versant in the economy of a family: That she shall have the charge of all the furniture and utensils in the house, according to an inventory, to be recorded in a book, of which a copy is always to be kept by the House Sub-Committee; and as new furniture or utensils are got, they must be added to the inventory: That she shall watch over the conduct of the girls and women servants in the house, and reprove and correct them for their faults: That she shall order the daily diet of the family, according to established rules: That she shall take care that the girls be employed in spinning, sewing, lace-working, knitting, or such other work as they are capable to perform; and that they attend the school regularly: That every thing in the house shall be kept clean and in good order: That she shall receive regulations for her conduct from the Managers, who, upon her failure or neglect, may admonish, and, if they find cause, suspend her from her office: That

F

she shall have such salary as shall be deemed proper by the Corporation or the Managers.

XIV. *Children.*

THAT the meeting of the Corporation, to be held on the second Monday of February yearly, may elect into the hospital as many children, boys or girls, as they judge the revenue of the Corporation is able, from time to time, to maintain; and the meeting, to be held on the second Monday of August, may supply any vacancies, arising from children, elected in February, not coming into the house: That no children shall be chosen who are under seven, or above eleven years of age: That no children shall be proposed to, or chosen by the said meetings, unless a document of their age, and a certificate of their circumstances, by the Minister or Kirk-Session of the parish where they reside, or by some other persons of credit, shall be laid before the Managers, at least one month before the election; and that, before they be admitted, they shall be inspected by the surgeon of the hospital, who must attest that they are healthy, and free from every infectious distemper and incurable disease: That all the children admitted into the hospital, shall have their lodging, diet, washing, linen, clothing, medicines, and education, in the said hospital, agreeably to the rules and practice of the same: That the boys and girls shall be uniformly apparelled in frugal and decent clothing, such as the Managers shall from time to time appoint: That if any of the children become turbulent, vicious, or disobedient to the Master or Mistress, they shall be corrected, or otherwise punished, or even expelled from the house, as the Managers shall see meet; and if any of them shall be afflicted with infectious diseases, the Managers shall order them to be boarded out of the house: That the children shall go out of the hospital at such time as shall be judged most expedient by the Managers, and shall then be put to apprenticeships or services.

XV. *Presentation of Children.*

THAT if any person shall give a benefaction of £200 sterling, or upwards, to be added to the stock of the Corporation, and shall be desirous of the privilege of presenting a Child to this Hospital, any quarterly meeting of the Corporation may, upon payment of the said sum to their Treasurer, make an act, giving and granting to such benefactor, and the heirs of his or her body; or to such series of heirs as shall be named in the deed of presentation, the perpetual power and privilege of presenting a Child, who shall be maintained, employed, and educated, according to the rules of the Hospital; provided always, That such Child shall be qualified and certified in manner set forth in the preceding byelaw: That whenever a child so presented and admitted is to be put out of, or removed from the Hospital, the person having the right of presentation as above, shall have the privilege of presenting another child, in common form; but reserving a power to the Corporation to redeem such rights of presentation, upon repayment of the said £200.

XVI. *Charter Chest.*

THAT there shall be three several locks and keys upon the charter-chest, or repositories, in which the writings, and other securities belonging to the Corporation, are lodged; of which keys, one shall be kept by the President of the Managers, another by the Treasurer, and the third by the Comptroller, all for the time being: That notes in writing shall be left in the charter chest, setting forth what papers have been taken out or put in, and for what purpose they have been taken out.

XVII. *Oath de Fideli.*

THAT all the officers of the Corporation, and every member that shall be assumed, shall give an oath of fidelity at their admission.

XVIII. *Mode of making new Bye-laws.*

THAT when it may be thought proper to amend or repeal any of the bye-laws of this Corporation, or to make new bye-laws, the overtures thereof shall be duly considered by the Managers, and then be laid before a quarterly meeting of the Corporation, who, after considering the same, shall refer them to the next quarterly meeting; which last meeting may either approve or disapprove of the said overtures as they shall think just.

No. III.

ORIGINAL GOVERNORS,

APPOINTED AUGUST 2, 1733.

The Right Hon. the Lord President of the Court of Session, and any other of the Lords of Session to be named by the Court

The Right Hon. the Lord Justice Clerk

The Right Hon. the Lord Advocate for Scotland

The Right Hon. the Lord Chief Baron of the Court of Exchequer

The Right Hon. the Lord Provost of Edinburgh

The Lord Dean of Guild

The Treasurer for the City of Edinburgh

The Solicitor-General for Scotland

The Dean of the Faculty of Advocates, and any other of the Faculty to be named by them

The Keeper of his Majesty's Signet, and any other Member of the Society of Writers to the Signet to be named by them

The Moderator of the Presbytery of Edinburgh, and any other Minister of the Presbytery, and a Ruling Member, to be named by them

The Principal of the University of Edinburgh, and any other to
  be named by the Masters thereof
The Preses of the College of Physicians
The Deacon-Convener of the Trades, and other two Deacons to
  be named by the rest
All the Trustees for Fisheries and Manufactures
The Master of the Merchant Company of Edinburgh
The Right Hon. Charles, Lord Cathcart
The Right Hon. Francis, Lord Napier
Charles Maitland of Pitrichie
Robert Craigie of Glendoich
Alexander Boswell, younger of Auchinleck
Alexander Learmonth, merchant, Edinburgh
William Henderson, do. do.
John Murray, do. do.
Alexander Young, writer, do.
Thomas Trotter, merchant, do.
Thomas Gardner, do. do.
William Braidwood, candlemaker, do.
Robert Fleeming, printer, do.
Thomas Lumsden, do. do.
James Wilson, smith, do.
All the Members of the Society in Scotland for propagating Chris-
  tian Knowledge

ASSUMED IN 1734.

The Rev. John Goudie, minister of Edinburgh
The Rev. George Logan, do. do.
The Rev. Patrick Cumming, do. do.
The Rev. John Glen, do. do.
Thomas Fenton, Bailie of Edinburgh
John Cochran, do. do.
Charles Crokatt, do. do.
John Brown, tailor, Edinburgh
Alexander Meason, merchant, do.
Robert Murray, do. do.
Andrew Dennet, do. do.
John Deans, surgeon, do.
Hugh Wilson, merchant, do.
George Mackie, do. do.
John Briggs, do. do.
Thomas Tulloch, writer, do.
George Hogg, brewer, do.
James Justice of Crichton
William Elder, stabler, Edinburgh
James Deans, tailor, do.
William Moffat, candlemaker, do.

William Adam, architect, Edinburgh
Thomas Heriot, one of the Bailies of do.
1735 Lord Alexander Hay
Alexander Wilson, brewer, Edinburgh
Robert Montgomerie, do. do.
William Walker, writer, do.
Maurice Cairns, brewer, do.
William Muir, merchant, do.
James Wood, do. do.
John Stewart, sen. do. do.
William Wright, baker, do.
John Thomson, do. do.
Robert Beatson, do. do.
John Wilson, timber merchant, do.
John Syme, slater, do.
John Wishart, shoemaker, do.
The Right Honourable the Earl of Hopetoun
The Moderator of the Synod of Lothian and Tweeddale
The Moderator of the Synod of Merse and Teviotdale
James Hunter, wright, Edinburgh
Patrick Campbell, baker, do.
Thomas Bell, do. do.
Michael Menzies, advocate, do.
Dr. John Riddell, physician, do.
William Hunter, merchant, do.
William Hamilton, brewer, do.
1736 James Bain, gardener, do.
John Inglis, timber merchant, do.
John Stewart, W. S. do.
Andrew Gardner, brewer, Burrowloch
John M'Goun, W. S. Edinburgh
Archibald Cockburn, merchant, do.
Archibald Stewart, W. S. do.
Daniel Campbell of Shawfield
Sir John Clerk of Pennicuik, Bart.
William Grant, advocate
Patrick Haldane, do.
Sir William Baird, Bart.
William Robertson, W. S.
James Burn, wright, Edinburgh
George Miller, merchant, do.
Allan Beg, do. do.
Thomas Elliot, writer, do.
George Wight, glazier, do.
The Rev. William Robertson, one of the ministers of Edinburgh
John Carlyle of Limekilns
1737 John Young, tailor, Canongate
James Milroy, timber merchant, Edinburgh
Robert Bull, do. do.

1737 David Dovie, architect, Edinburgh
1738 The Hon. John Hay of Lawfield
     Alexander Wight, tenant in Cousland
1739 Robert Inglis, merchant, Edinburgh
     Alexander Stevenson, of Mountgreenan, W. S.
     Andrew Thomson, brewer, Edinburgh
     David Berry, merchant, do.
     Thomas Rigg of Morton, advocate
     The Rev. Robert Wallace, Edinburgh
     Alexander Monro, surgeon, do.
     Hugh Murray of Kinninmonth, advocate
     William Alexander, merchant, Edinburgh
     James Armour, writer, do.
     John Coutts, merchant, do.
     James Stewart, merchant, Edinburgh
     James Stirling, do. do.
     Allan Whitefield, Receiver-General of Land Tax
     Alexander Dundas, merchant, London
1740 Gilbert Laurie, surgeon, Edinburgh
     John Bell, brewer, do.
     Peter Scott, do. do.
     James Dundas, physician, do.
1741 James Nimmo, merchant, do.
     Archibald Wallace, do. do.
     Alexander Christie, do. do.
     Rev. Alexander Webster, one of the ministers of do.
     Hew Crawford, writer, do.
     Yaxly Davidson, weaver, do.

MEMBERS NOMINATED BY THE PATENT.

The Lord Justice-General for Scotland
The Lord President of the Court of Session
The Senior Senator of the College of Justice
His Majesty's Advocate for Scotland
The Lord Justice Clerk
The Lord Chief Baron of Exchequer
The Senior Baron of that Court
The Lord Provost of Edinburgh
The Dean of Guild and Treasurer
His Majesty's Solicitor for Scotland
The Dean of the Faculty of Advocates
The Treasurer to the said Faculty
The Keeper of his Majesty's Signet in Scotland
The Treasurer to the Society of Clerks to his Majesty's Signet
The Senior Commissioner for the said Society
The Moderator of the Presbytery of Edinburgh
The Senior Minister of the City of Edinburgh
The Principal of the University of Edinburgh
The Professor of Divinity in the said University

The Preses of the Royal College of Physicians
The Professor of Anatomy in the said University
The Master of the Merchant Company, Edinburgh
The Deacon Convener of the Trades of do.
The Deacon of the Surgeons, do.
The Deacon of the Weavers, do.
    All for the time being, and their successors.

ALSO,

John Earl of Hopetoun
Patrick Campbell of Monzie, one of the Senators of the College
    of Justice
William Carmichael of Skirling, Bart.
Sir Gilbert Elliot of Stobs, Bart.
John Erskine of Carnoch
Daniel Campbell of Shawfield
George Buchan, of Camledge
James Nimmo, Receiver-General of Excise
Patrick Haldane of Bearcrofts, advocate
Alexander Boswell of Auchinleck, do.
Rev. George Logan, Edinburgh
Rev. Alexander Webster, do.
Rev. John Hepburn, do.
Dr. James Dundas, physician, do.
Dr. James Boswell, do. do.
Thomas Dundas of Fingask, merchant, do.
Alexander Arbuthnot, of Knox, do. do.
John Cochran of Alderstoun, do. do.
John Coutts, do. do.
John Wilson, do. do.
George Millar, do. do.
William Hamilton, brewer, do.
Alexander Young, writer, do.
Alexander Christie, do. do.
Robert Tod, merchant, do.
Archibald Wallace, do. do.
John Inglis, do. do.
William Braidwood, candlemaker, Edinburgh
John Young, taylor, do.
John Murray, merchant, do.
William Henderson, do. do.
Gilbert Lawrie, surgeon apothecary, do.
Robert Fleming, printer, do.
Thomas Gairdner, merchant, do.
Alexander Chalmers, do. do.
Archibald Cockburn, do. do.
Alexander Stevenson of Mountgreenan, W. S.
Hugh Crawfurd, W. S.

William Millar, W. S.
John Paton, bookseller, Edinburgh
Nicol Spence, writer, do.
William Robertson of Falside, W. S.
William Hog, merchant, Edinburgh
Thomas Trotter, do. do.
James Milroy, do. do.
Andrew Thomson, brewer, do.
James Stirling, merchant, do.
John Forrest, do. do.
Thomas Lumsden, printer, do.
Archibald Stewart, merchant, do.
Alexander Mason, do. do.
John Kennedy, surgeon apothecary, do.
George Cunninghame, do. do.
William Wardrobe, do. do.
John Wallace, do. do.
Alexander Alison, Deputy Receiver of Excise
William Walker, writer, Edinburgh
William Adam, architect, do.
James Wilson, Smith, do.

MEMBERS OF THE INCORPORATION ASSUMED.

1743 The Hon. Lord Napier, Senator of the College of Justice
The Hon. Lord Balmerino, do.
The Hon. Lord Dunn, do.
The Hon. Lord Drummore, do.
The Hon. Lord Kilkerran, do.
The Hon. Lord Murkle, do.
The Hon. John Hay of Lawfield
The Hon. Charles Erskine of Edenshead
Joseph Williamson, advocate
Thomas Hope of Rankeillour, do.
Michael Menzies, do.
Charles Maitland of Pitrichie, do.
Colonel James Gardner, do.
James Baillie of Hardington, W. S.
Alexander M'Millan of Drumore, do.
John Dundas of Newhalls, do.
Archibald Campbell, do.
Alexander Campbell, do.
John M'Gowan, do.
David Dickson, writer, Edinburgh
David Anderson, do. do.
Thomas Tullich, do. do.
James Watson of Ormiston, do. do.
Rev. William Gushart
Rev. Neil Macvicar
Rev. James Walker
Rev. George Wishart

Rev. William Robertson
Rev. Robert Hamilton
Rev. Robert Wallace
Rev. John Glen
Rev. James Bannatyne
Rev. Robert Kinloch
Rev. Peter Cumming
Rev. James Nisbet
Rev. William Harper, episcopal clergyman
Rev. Robert Blair, do.
Rev. William Hunter, do.
Rev. Robert Keith, do.
Robert Ferguson of Raith
George Preston, druggist
Thomas Crokat, merchant
Thomas Heriot, do.
James Stewart, sen. do.
John Stewart, do.
Allan Begg, do.
Robert Frier, do.
William Alexander, do.
Robert Englis, do.
Peter Crichton, do.
Alexander Lamond, do.
John Mackie, do.
Thomas Ruddiman, keeper of the Advocates' Library
James Davidson of Halltree
John Traill, bookseller
John Oswald, do. London
William Elder, stabler
Robert Montgomery, brewer
Andrew Gairdner, do.
Patrick Scott, do.
Maurice Cairns, do.
James Bain of Bainfield
David Dowie, architect
James Hunter, wright
James Heriot, do.
John Thomson, baker
Robert Beatson, do.
William Wight, do.
John Wisbart, cordiner
William Dickson, dyer
Thomas Miln, mason
Patrick Lawson, weaver
James Brown, do.
1747 Robert Baillie, merchant
1748 Andrew Chalmers, writer

G

1749 Alexander Lindsay, merchant
    Robert Forrester, do.
    James Grant, do.
    John Dunsmuir, do.
    Patrick Bowie, do.
    Reverend James Stevenson, Edinburgh
1750 James Smollet, advocate
    John Mein, slater
1751 James Napier, merchant
    Reverend George Key, West-Kirk
    Thomas Trotter, younger, merchant
    William Ramsay
1753 Robert Ferguson of Raith
    George Chalmers, merchant
    James Carmichael, writer to the signet
    John Hope, merchant
    William Govan, glazier
    Richard Lothian, writer
    Robert Wight, merchant
1754 John Mathie, weaver
1755 James Beveridge, merchant
    Andrew Jamieson, do.
    Robert Smith, surgeon
1756 John Caw, Excise-Office
1757 Bailie John Walker
1758 Robert M'Farlane, Cashier Insurance Office
    Walter Scott, baker
    John Thomson, Excise
1759 Reverend George Whitfield
    Walter Corser, writing-master
    George Reith, weaver
    James Gentle, brewer
1760 James Thomson, merchant
1763 Robert Alexander, do.
1764 Robert Scott Moncreiff of Rhind
1765 William Galloway, merchant
1766 Robert Jamieson, writer
    Rev. John Erskine, Edinburgh
    Rev. James Bayne, relief minister
1767 John Lockhart of Lee
    James Thomson, accountant of excise
    Rev. George Barclay, Haddington
1768 David Moncreiff, advocate
    Roger Robertson, younger of Ladykirk
    Rev. Joseph Townsend, Pewsey
    William Murray, merchant
1769 John M'Lean, do.
1770 William Tod, do.
    Anthony Ferguson, do.
    Alexander Crichton, coach-wright

1771 James Sym, slater
1772 David Smith, baker
     Charles Wallace, merchant
     James Young, wigmaker
     Rev. John Gibson, West Kirk
     Robert Scyth, upholsterer
1773 The Earl of Breadalbane
     Alexander Belches, advocate
     Robert Wight, baker
     Dr. John Hope, physician
     James Forrest of Comiston
     John Dundas of Duddingston
     Sir James Adolphus Oughton
     James Balfour of Pilrig
     William Binning, Esq.
     Alexander Mowbray, merchant
     Alexander Bell, merchant
     Sir William Forbes, Bart.
     James Donaldson, printer
     William Anderson, saddler
     Daniel Millar, merchant
     William Burn, do.
1775 Dr. Thomas Glen, physician
1776 Rev. Thomas Davidson, Braintree
     Thomas Boyes, writer
     The Earl of Hyndford
     John Bonnar, painter
     Professor Robertson
1777 Lord Hope
     John Belches of Invermay
     Rev. Mr. Finlay, Dollar
     Walter Russell, merchant
     John Paterson, tailor
1778 James Dinwiddie, Manchester
     John Campbell, W. S.
1779 Rev. Sir Henry Moncreiff Wellwood, Bart.
     Patrick Wallace of Latour
     William M'Lean, merchant
     Thomas Hutchison, do.
     Thomas Tod, do.
     Dr. Gregory Grant, physician
     Thomas Belches of Greenyards
     John Fletcher, baker
     Rev. Robert Walker, Edinburgh
     Rev. John Kemp, do.
     Rev. Thomas Randall, do.
     Rev. David Johnston, Leith
1780 Richard Lake, writer
     Christopher Mowbray, Edinburgh

Christopher Cameron, tailor
Alexander Dickie, clockmaker
1781 Rev. Dr Robert Henry, Edinburgh
Dr Andrew Duncan, Physician
Henry Mackenzie, Exchequer
Neil MacVicar, manufacturer
Thomas Ruthven, writer
Peter Crawford
Robert Young upholsterer
Edward Lothian
John Gloag, merchant
1782 James Home Rigg of Morton
James Mitchell, merchant, Leith
Samuel Mitchelson, junior, W.S.
Robert Young, merchant
Dr Charles Stuart, physician
Francis Braidwood, wright
1783 John Moncreiff, apothecary
*Rev. T. S. Jones, Lady Glenorchy's Chapel
James Forrest, W.S.
1784 Robert Belches of Greenyards
James Walker, W.S.
Benjamin Bell, surgeon
Alexander Allan, merchant
Patrick Miller, banker
Alexander Houston, do.
Alexander Bonar, do.
John Tawse, writer
Isaac Grant, W.S.
1785 James Ogilvy, Customs
Rev. James Brown, Edinburgh
Horatius Canning, W.S.
John Hutton, stationer
James Jackson, merchant
Andrew Hamilton, comptroller, Excise
Rev. Dr William Gloag, Edinburgh.
1786 Rev. Dr Hugh Blair, Edinburgh
Rev. Dr. John Drysdale, do.
Rev. William Greenfield, do.
William Ramsay, banker
Rev. William Simpson, Greenlaw
John Lothian, merchant
William Patison, do.
1787 Right Hon. Lord Balgonie
Thomas Cumming, banker
Elphinston Balfour, bookseller
David Steuart, banker
Robert Allan, do.

1787 Rev. Dr. Abernethy Drummond
Dr William Laing, physician
John Veitch, marble-cutter
John Tod of Kirklands
Rev. James Brown, Newbattle
Robert Brown, W.S.
Thomas Brown, merchant
James Brown, junior, staymaker
George Kinnear, banker
Rev. William Moodie, Edinburgh
1788 James Stirling, banker
Charles Robertson, painter
William M'Donald, W.S.
James Simpson, stationer
James Cargill, merchant
Dr. Nathan Spens, physician
John Balfour, bookseller
James Morrison, merchant, Leith
Rev. George Hill, St. Andrews
William Simpson, cashier, Royal Bank
Alexander Forbes
John Black, merchant
Peter Forrester, do.
1789 The Hon. Henry Erskine
David Cleghorn, brewer
*Robert Sym, W. S.
John Scoular, merchant
*Rev. Dr. G. H. Baird, Edinburgh
1790 John Wauchope, W. S.
*Andrew Blane, W. S.
1791 *Rev. Thomas M'Knight, Leith
Adam Rolland, advocate.
James Carfrae, merchant
Allan Maconochie, advocate
James Balvaird, Excise
William Coulter, hosier
Andrew Kinnear, pewterer
1792 William Hope Weir of Craigiehall
Rev. Dr. Thomas Hardie, Edinburgh
1793 Archibald Campbell, younger of Clathick
Alexander Wood, surgeon
*Thomas Cranstoun, W. S.
Rev. James Finlayson, Edinburgh
Walter Wood, merchant
1794 Rev. Henry David Hill, North Berwick
1795 Rev. Robert Walker, Canongate
1796 Rev. Walter Buchannan, do.
John Pitcairn, merchant
Alexander Pitcairn, do.

1796 David Thomson, do.
    Rev. David Black, Edinburgh
    James Hamilton, upholsterer
1798 *Rev. Dr. Robert Lorimer, Haddington
    William Beveridge, W. S.
1799 *William Scott Moncrieff, accountant
    *Robert Scott Moncrieff, merchant
    Thomas Scotland, W. S.
    Captain Forbes Drummond, R. N.
    Rev. Archibald Bonar, Cramond
    William Creech, bookseller
    Richard Douglas, George Square
    William Aitchison, jeweller
    Samuel Anderson, banker
    James Bonar, solicitor of excise
1800 James Mansfield, banker
    Sir John Hay, Bart. do.
    Andrew Bonar, do.
    George Ramsay, do.
    William Ramsay, jun. do.
    *William Kerr, secretary, General Post Office
    George White, merchant
    Ebenezer Mason, do.
    Rev. William Paul, St. Cuthberts
    James Bruce, accountant, Excise
    Count Rumford
    *Rev. Andrew Brown, D.D. Edinburgh
1801 Alexander Duncan, W. S.
    Rev. William Bennet, Duddingston
    Archibald Burnet, Edinburgh
    Captain Ninian Louis, do.
    Archibald Menzies, merchant
    Captain James Tod, Edinburgh
1802 Rev. W. F. Ireland, Leith
    Hon. Baron Clerk Rattray
    *Alexander Osborn, Customs
    William Oliphant, Leith
    Rev. Robert Balfour, Glasgow
1803 Robert Anderson, merchant
    *Rev. Dr. Robert Anderson, Edinburgh
1804 Rev. Dr. John Thomson, do.
    *Rev. Henry Grey, Stenton
    Hugh Warrender, W. S.
    *James Forrest of Comiston
    James Dundas, W. S.
1805 *John Wardrop, banker
    William Brown, surgeon
    *Robert Plenderleath, merchant
    Charles Watson, upholsterer

1806 *Rev. Dr. Alexander Brunton, Edinburgh
    John Muir, merchant
    *Rev. Dr. David Dickson, St. Cuthbert's
1807 Sir William Forbes, Bart.
    William Trotter of Ballendean
    *Robert Scott, apothecary
    Thomas Hogg of Newliston
    Archibald Geddes, Leith
    Patrick Crichton, coachmaker
    Rev. Dr. John Campbell, Edinburgh
    *James Walker, merchant, Leith
1808 James Neilson of Millbank
    Samuel Paterson, merchant
    Rev. Dr. Thomas Fleming, Edinburgh
1809 Rev. Dr. James Robertson, Leith
    George Brunton, merchant
1810 Rev. Dr. Andrew Thomson, Edinburgh
    *Andrew Gairdner, merchant
    James Robertson, do.
1811 *John Waugh, bookseller
    *Rev. Dr. David Ritchie, Edinburgh
1812 *Robert Stevenson, civil-engineer
    Rev. David Dickson, Edinburgh
    *William Whyte, bookseller
    Gilbert Innes of Stow
    *William Gallaway, merchant
    Robert Reid, architect
    Alexander Laing, do.
1814 Robert Menzies, shipbuilder, Leith
1815 *Rev. Walter Tait, Edinburgh
1816 *Rev. Angus Makellar, Pencaitland
    Sir Henry Raeburn, Knt.
1817 *Rev. Dr. Andrew Grant, Edinburgh
    *Walter Brown, merchant
1818 *George Ross, advocate
1819 *William Murray, banker
    *Dr. John Abercromby, physician
    *Rev. Charles Watson, Burntisland
1820 William Thomson, banker
    *Robert Paul, do.
    *John Tawse, advocate
    *Rev. Dr. George Muirhead, Cramond
1821 *Sir Samuel Shepherd, Bart. Lord Chief Baron
1822 *Adam Duff, Sheriff of Edinburgh
    *Sir Henry Jardine, Knight
    Francis Nalder, merchant
    *Rev. Dr. John Lee, Edinburgh
1823 Rev. Dr. George Wright, Stirling
    *John Mackenzie, glazier

1823 *Dr. James Buchan, physician
1824 *John Dunlop, Edinburgh
    *Rev. Dr. Robert Gordon, do.
    *Sir Robert Liston
    *John Bonar of Ratho
    *William Bonar, banker
    Charles Tawse, W.S.
    *Andrew Tawse, W.S.
1825 *Rev. Dr. William Muir, Edinburgh
1826 *Rev. James Henderson, Stockbridge Chapel
    *Thomas Miller, glover
    *Dr. William Brown, surgeon
    *Dr. William Moncreiff, physician
1827 *John S. More, advocate
    *Rev. John Purves, Lady Glenorchy's Chapel
    *John Lyall, merchant
    *Sir Patrick Walker, Knt.
    *William Alexander, merchant, Leith
    *John Bonar of Kimmerghame
    *Andrew Bonar, banker
    *Dr. James Begbie, surgeon
1828 *Walter Dickson, W. S.
    *Mungo Ponton, W. S.
    *William Young, W. S.
    *John Elder, W. S.
    *Joseph Liddell, S. S. C.
    *Dr. William Beilby, physician
    *Claud Muirhead, printer
    *John Lauder, merchant
    *William Fleming, banker
    *William Paul, accountant
    *James Howden, jeweller
    *Dr. W. P. Alison, physician
    *Walter Jollie, W. S.
    *John Hope, Esq. Dean of the Faculty of Advocates
    *James Hope, W. S.
    *Andrew Storie, W. S.
    *John Russell, W. S.
    *Vans Hathorn, W. S.
    *John Thomson, cashier, Royal Bank
    *Rev. John Forbes, Hope Park Chapel
1829 Thomas Kinnear, banker
    *Rev, James Marshall, Edinburgh
    *Archibald Scott, solicitor.
    *Archibald Bonar, Royal Bank
    *William Pitt Dundas, advocate
1830 *David Thomson, W. S.
    *Rev. James Martin, Stockbridge Chapel
    *Sir John Stuart Forbes, Bart.

1830 * David Anderson of Moredun, banker
    *George Forbes, banker
1831 *Adam Hay, do.
    *James Bonar, W. S.
    *William Bonar, junr. banker
    *Thomas Jones, do. Leith
    Thomas Allan, banker
    *Rev. James Begg, Lady Glenorchy's Chapel
    *Robert Bell, advocate
    *William Ellis, S.S.C.
    *Robert Fleming, brewer
    *William Innes, W. S.
1832 *J. R. Sibbald, surgeon
    *David George Sandeman of Springlands
    *John Leithead, attorney, Alnwick
    *Thomas Hamilton, architect
✗ *Rev. William Scott Moncrieff, Penicuik
1833 *George Smyth, advocate
    *Charles Ferguson, younger of Kilkerran, do.
    *Adam Anderson, advocate
    *Graham Speirs, do.
    *Rev. John Paul, St. Cuthbert's
    *Joseph Murray of Ayton

The surviving Members are Marked *

No. IV.

DONORS,

Who have given £10 and upwards to the Funds of the Hospital. To have inserted Donations below that sum would have swelled this list to an improper length.

Those establishing presentations are marked *

1733 Mr. Nicol Spence, agent for the Church of Scotland	£10	0	0
1734 Right Hon. Janet Countess of Wemyss	-	-	10	0	0
Right Hon. Lord Alexander Hay	-	-	10	0	0
Right Hon. Adam Cockburn, Lord Justice Clerk	10	0	0
Thomas Heriot, Esq. one of the Magistrates of Edinburgh - - - - -	20	0	0
Mr. Alexander Brown, pewterer in do. - -	11	2	2
Mr. William Muir, merchant - - - -	10	0	0
Mr. Andrew Dennet, do. - - - - -	10	0	0

Year	Name	£	s	d
1735	Right Hon. Charles Earl of Hopetoun	100	0	0
	Right Hon. Sir Hew Dalrymple, Bart. Lord President	30	0	0
	Hon. Patrick Campbell of Monzie, one of the Senators of the College of Justice	50	0	0
	Hon. Hew Dalrymple of Drummore, do.	10	0	0
	Hon. James Elphingston of Coupar, do.	10	0	0
	Hon. Sir Gilbert Elliot of Minto, Bart. do.	10	0	0
	Hon. Andrew Fletcher of Milton, do.	10	0	0
	Hon. Alexander Fraser of Strichen, do.	10	0	0
	Hon. Patrick Grant of Elchies, do.	10	0	0
	Hon. John Sinclair of Murkle, do.	10	0	0
	Charles Areskine of Barjarg, Solicitor-General	10	0	0
1736	Sir William Baird of Newbyth, Bart.	25	0	0
	*Captain Dougal Campbell of Inveraw. In Royal Bank Stock	500	0	0
1737	His Grace Charles, Duke of Queensberry and Dover	10	10	0
	Sir John Anstruther, Bart.	10	0	0
	John Anderson of St. Christophers, M. D.	100	0	0
	Daniel Campbell of Shawfield, Esq.	50	0	0
	Mr. William Drummond, W. S.	20	0	0
1738	Sir James Rochead of Inverleith, Bart.	200	0	0
	Lady Orbiston, (being Assembly Money)	59	6	3
	Mrs. Andrew Dennet	11	2	2
	Mrs. Mary Johnston, Edinburgh	21	6	3
1739	Mrs. Wightman of Mauldslie	20	0	0
	Mr. James Wilson, smith	24	11	0
	Mrs. John Plenderleath,	11	18	0
	Robert Ferguson of Raith, Esq.	10	0	0
1740	Right Hon. William Earl of Aberdeen	20	0	0
	Right Hon. Countess Dowager of Bute	20	0	0
	Mrs. Elizabeth Erskine	119	8	10
	Mrs. Ann M'Ilwraith, Edinburgh	250	0	0
	Archibald Cockburn of Cockpen, Esq.	13	3	0
	Mr. William Moffat, Candlemaker	41	16	6
	Mrs. Elisabeth Kilgour	40	0	0
1740	Mrs. Margaret Ker, Edinburgh	16	13	4
1741	Her Grace the Duchess Dowager of Gordon	10	5	0
	Mr. Andrew Gairdner, Treasurer to the Hospital	108	4	2
	Mrs. Gairdner, his widow	20	0	0
	John Coutts, Esq. afterwards Lord Provost of Edinburgh	15	5	0
	Colonel James Gardner	12	18	0
1742	Mrs. Durham of Duntarvie	113	14	4
	Captain Alexander Horn	100	0	0
	John Cramond, hair-merchant, Edinburgh, under certain burdens and annuities	370	10	6
	Mrs. Bannatyne of Edinburgh	10	0	0

Year	Donor	£	s	d
1742	Alexander Johnston of Straton, Esq.	10	0	0
1743	Mrs. Garden of Troup	27	15	6
	Mrs. Janet Aitken, widow. of Rev. D. Aitken, Wooller	10	0	0
1744	*Right Hon. Henrietta, Countess-Dowager of Hopetoun	100	0	0
	Mrs. Thomas Muschet	62	2	0
	Mr. William Wilson, merchant	32	5	10
	Mr. John Brown, tailor	17	15	9
	Mr. Robert Grier, merchant	10	0	0
1745	Robert Murray of Murrayshall, Esq.	20	0	0
	Mrs William Ewing	11	2	2
	Mrs Campbell of Finab	10	0	0
	Mr Alexander Bruce, merchant	10	15	10
1746	Robert Purves, Esq. late one of the Magistrates of Edinburgh	30	0	0
1747	George Cruickshanks, Esq. general examiner of customs	66	13	4
	Mrs Isabel French, Edinburgh	10	10	0
	Mrs Handasyde, do.	10	0	0
1748	Anthony Murray of Balmanno, Esq.	54	5	6
	Mrs Francis Archibald, widow of the Rev. Mr Archibald, formerly master of the Hospital	27	15	6
	Mrs Margaret Smith, Stamp Office, Edinburgh	10	0	0
1749	Mr John Murray, merchant, in several donations	11	0	6
1750	Mr Robert Pringle, writer	55	0	0
1751	Mr John Young, tailor	162	11	10
	Right Hon. Countess of Glencairn, (being Assembly money)	31	9	1
1752	Sir Gilbert Elliot of Stobs, Bart.	40	5	0
1754	Mr John Gordon, late Factor to the Earl of Hopetoun	100	0	0
	Mr Colin Drummond, Professor of Philosophy	11	13	4
1756	James Dundas, M. D. in several donations	118	0	0
	James Carmichael of Hales, do.	16	6	0
1757	Right Hon. the Countess of Cassilis	10	0	0
	*Mrs Christian Pringle	122	4	5
	Mr Thomas Lumsden, printer, in several donations	93	19	0
	Mr Gilbert Laurie, surgeon, do.	14	0	0
	Mr James Nimmo, cashier of excise, do.	12	10	0
	Mrs Margaret Nicol, Edinburgh	10	0	0
1758	Mr Samuel Walker of Exeter	20	0	0
1759	Mr John Brown of Lasswade	100	0	0
	Mrs Captain Clerk	111	2	2
	Mr William Monro, bookseller	28	15	0
	Hon. Wm. Carmichael of Skirling, in several donations	25	0	0
1760	Alexander Arbuthnot of Knox, Esq.	100	0	0
1761	George Buchan of Kello, Esq. in several donations	37	2	0
	Mr Archd. Wallace, merchant, do.	10	15	6
1762	*Mrs Barbara Dundas, widow of Alexander Irving of Saphock, Esq.	300	0	0

Year	Donor	£	s	d
1763	Right Hon. William Earl of Fife	25	0	6
	Mr John Mitchell, farmer, Windlestrawlee	50	0	6
	Miss Forbes of Ballogie	20	0	0
	Mr Robert Alexander, merchant	12	12	6
	Mr John Hope, do. in several donations	11	11	0
1765	Rev. William Brown, Edinburgh	56	1	6
	Patrick Wallace, Esq. Arbroath, in several donations	15	15	0
	The Bounty of the Trustees for Manufactures from the year 1735	521	17	0
1766	Rev. William Harper, in several donations	23	14	6
	Mr John Chenybow, barber	11	0	0
1767	Alexander Barclay of Jamaica, M. D.	50	0	0
	Mr. Thomas Fraser, writer, Edinburgh	30	0	0
	Mrs. Katharine Lawson, do.	10	0	0
1768	Mr. Thomas Coterell	100	0	0
	Rev. George Whitfield, various collections	1592	0	0
1769	Rev. Jos. Townsend, do.	410	0	0
	Mr. Samuel Anderson, St. Clement Danes, London	113	17	7
1770	Lady Fraser of Dores	105	0	0
	Mr. P. Maclellan, son of Sir Samuel Maclellan, Lord Provost of Edinburgh	624	1	7
	Mr. Purdie, mason	31	15	6
	Mr. George Chalmers, merchant, in several donations	21	0	0
1773	James Forrest of Comiston, Esq.	100	0	0
1774	The Estate of Miss Martha Dalrymple, consisting of heritable subjects, situated in Charles Street, Edinburgh.			
1775	Right Hon. John Earl of Hopetoun	30	0	0
	Hon. Mrs. Carmichael of Saltcoats, in several donations	75	0	0
	John Lockhart of Lee, Esq. do.	45	0	0
	Rev. Thomas Davidson, Braintree, Essex	10	10	0
	David Hume, Esq. in several donations	15	0	0
	Thomas Glen, M. D.	10	0	0
	David Stuart Moncrieffe of Meredun, Esq. in several donations	27	0	0
1776	Right Hon. John, Earl of Breadalbane	21	0	0
	William Robertson of Ladykirk, Esq. in several donations	30	11	0
	James Smollet of Bonhill, Esq.	40	0	0
1777	John Bonnar, painter, in two donations	30	0	0
	Miss Euphan Murray	20	0	0
	J. Belches of Invermay	10	0	0
	Helenus Halkerston, Esq.	33	3	0
	Mrs Margaret Sprewel	10	0	0
	Countess Dowager of Balcarras	15	0	0
	Right Hon. Lord Belhaven	50	0	0
	Mrs Lockhart of Lee	10	0	0
	Mrs Butler, druggist	50	0	0

1777	The Trades of Leith, in two donations -	21	10	0
	*Mrs Elizabeth Carmichael - -	150	0	0
1778	John Dundas of Duddingston - -	110	0	0
1779	*Mrs Scott of Bellvue - - -	150	0	0
1780	Mrs Neilson - - - -	50	0	0
	Mrs Robb - - - -	50	0	0
1781	*Dr Gregory Grant - - -	150	0	0
	The Authors of the Mirror, per H. Mackenzie, Esq.	150	0	0
	Miss Keith - - -	10	0	0
	Mr James Grant - - -	20	0	0
	Mrs Hamilton of Biel - - -	20	0	0
	Sir Wm. Forbes, J. Hunter, and Co. -	15	15	0
	Samuel Mitchelson, Esq. - - -	21	0	0
	William Corrie, Willoughbrough - -	10	0	0
	Lord Auchinleck - - -	10	10	0
	Lady Lockhart Ross - - -	10	0	0
	William Davidson of Muirhouse - -	20	0	0
	Right Hon. Earl of Hopetoun - -	50	0	0
1782	Hon. Captain Napier - - -	50	0	0
	Her Grace the Duchess of Buccleuch -	21	0	0
	Dowager Lady Blantyre - -	20	0	0
	John Tod of Kirklands, in two donations -	20	0	0
1783	Dr James Johnstone - - -	20	0	0
	William Dickson - - -	35	0	0
	Robert Belsches, Esq. - - -	20	0	0
	Alexander Sbairp, London - -	10	10	0
1785	Misses Warrender - - - -	15	0	0
	Mrs Henrietta Thomson - - -	10	0	0
	Miss Wilkieson, Amsterdam - - -	10	0	0
1786	Miss Hope - - - -	11	9	5
	Mrs Miller, Montrose - - -	20	0	0
	Mr Johnston - - - -	20	0	0
	George Inglis, Esq. - - -	50	0	0
	Alexander Hunter, Esq. - - -	50	0	0
	Major William Sands - - -	10	0	0
1787	Captain Walter Riddell - - -	27	15	6
	Lady Glenorchy - - -	100	0	0
	Mrs Young - - - -	14	10	5
	Hugh Mosman, Esq. - - -	21	0	0
	Patrick Wallace, Esq. of Latour, in different donations, and a legacy - - -	333	0	0
	*Thomas Tod, Esq. late Treasurer to the Hospital, in donations and a legacy - -	1000	0	0
1788	William Ferguson, Esq. - -	50	0	0
1789	Mrs Gibson of Durie - - - -	50	0	0
	General John Houstoun - - -	20	0	0
	Miss Mary Douglas - - -	50	0	0
	James Home Rigg of Morton - -	111	2	2
	Right Hon. Earl of Breadalbane - - -	21	0	0

1702	Right Hon. Earl of Hyndford, in various annual do-			
	nations from 1777	530	0	0
	Baron Steuart Moncreiff, do. do.	540	0	0
	*Lady Charlotte Erskine	210	0	0
	Archibald Swinton, Esq.	10	0	0
	Mrs Campbell of Fairfield	20	0	0
	Captain Lockhart, R. N.	10	0	0
1790	Archbibald Campbell of Succoth	10	0	0
	Hon. John Grant, Chief Justice of Jamaica	15	0	0
	John Gordon of Balmuir	16	13	4
	Laurence Coulter, Esq. Glasgow	150	0	0
1791	John Balfour, bookseller	20	0	0
	William Binning, Esq.	50	0	0
	John Fyffe	50	0	0
	Mrs. Robb	50	0	0
1792	Henry Thornton, Esq.	20	0	0
	*Miss Grey of Teasses	200	0	0
	Dr James Laing	100	0	0
1794	Mrs. Agnes Dickson of Hartree	15	0	0
	Mrs. Fleming	10	0	0
	Miss Agnes Keith	100	0	0
	Mrs. Margaret Mitchell	10	0	0
1795	William Hunter, pewterer	50	0	0
	Mrs. Stewart, relict of W. Stewart, writer	50	0	0
	Mrs. General Houston	10	0	0
1796	Lord Gardenston	100	0	0
	A Lady, per Sir W. Forbes	25	0	0
	Mrs. Janet Threipland	10	0	0
	The Very Rev. Principal Baird	10	10	0
1797	Lady Campbell of Lochnell	40	0	0
	Alexander Forbes of Kirkpottie	10	0	0
	James Gillespie of Spylaw	100	0	0
	R. Gillespie	40	0	0
1798	Mrs. Isobel Mudie, relict of John Watson, W.S. un-			
	der the burden of an annuity of £5	181	4	9
	Mrs. Beath	20	0	0
	Mrs. Lockhart	100	0	0
	Mrs. Scotland	50	0	0
	Bishop Abernethy Drummond, in several donations	100	0	0
1799	John Tod, Esq.	100	0	0
	Mr. Kinloch of Kelvie	20	0	0
	Captain James Drysdale	100	0	0
	William Stewart, writer	50	0	0
1800	Mrs. Smyth of Methven	50	0	0
	Laurence Coulter, Esq. Glasgow	150	0	0
1801	Lady Christian Graham	200	0	0
	John Richardson of Pitfour	10	0	0
	The Countess of Hyndford	20	0	0
	Sir John Callander	10	10	0
1802	Mrs. Jean Ormiston	30	0	0
	*Miss Alison Lothian	200	0	0

Year	Donor	£	s.	d.
1802	The Barons of Exchequer from the effects of James Edwards - - - -	10	10	0
1803	Isaac Hawkins, Esq. £300 Consols, valued at -	180	0	0
	Mrs. Gordon - - -	20	0	0
	Charles Thomson, Esq. - - -	100	0	0
	Mrs. Janet Murray Keith - -	100	0	0
	Richard Douglas, Esq. in different donations -	57	0	0
1804	The Barons of Exchequer, from the estate of Thomas M'Glashan - - - -	32	18	6
	*Captain James Drysdale - - -	400	0	0
	The Barons of Exchequer from the estate of Catherine M'Intosh - - - -	50	0	0
1805	James Mitchell, Leith - - -	100	0	0
1806	Richard Dickson of Logiegreen - -	20	0	0
	Mrs. Agnes Millar - - -	10	0	0
1807	Thomas Hog of Newliston - - -	10	0	0
	William Peebles, late master of the Hospital -	50	0	0
	Sir William Forbes, Bart. of Pitsligo - -	200	0	0
	Mrs. Kerr, the fourth part of a house, producing	21	2	6
1808	Mrs. Commissioner Grieve - -	100	0	0
	Anonymous, from Inverness - -	40	0	0
1809	The Parish of Ratho - - -	25	0	0
	Miss Somerville of Fingask - - -	10	0	0
1810	The Barons of Exchequer, on an application from the Managers, from the estate of Richard Douglas, educated in the Hospital under burden of an annuity of £75 - - - - -	2500	0	0
	Convener Andrew Gairdner - - -	10	10	0
	Miss Macpherson's Boarding School - -	10	0	0
1811	Miss Porterfield - - - -	20	0	0
	William Swanson, writing-master - -	10	0	0
	Rev. George Bruce, late minister of Dunbar -	315	6	6
	Robert Stevenson, civil engineer - -	31	10	0
	Allan Begg, accountant of excise - -	10	0	0
	The Barons of Exchequer, from the estate of the late Lieut.-Colonel Duncan Campbell - -	27	7	2
1812	H. Mitchell, Esq. - - -	70	4	5
1813	Dr Joseph Robertson - - -	20	0	0
	Her Grace the Duchess Dowager of Buccleuch -	12	12	0
	Gilbert Innes, Esq. of Stow - -	10	10	0
	William Galloway, insurance broker - -	10	10	0
	Hon. Lord Craigie - - -	50	0	0
1815	Mr. Jameson Durham, of Duntarvie -	110	0	0
	Robert Scott Moncrieff, Esq. - -	10	0	0
1817	John Wauchope, Esq. W.S. - - -	20	0	0
	*John Fullerton of Carberry, Esq. - -	500	0	0
1819	Rev. Charles Watson - - -	21	0	0
	Alexander Bonar, Esq. of Ratho - -	21	0	0
	Andrew Mein, Esq. - - -	30	0	0

Year	Name	£	s	d
1819	A Gentleman	50	0	0
1820	Robert Young, Esq. Queen Street	100	0	0
	Mr. Hutchison, flesher	200	0	0
	Mrs. Begg, James' Square	100	0	0
	James Forrest, Esq. of Comiston	100	0	0
	George White, merchant	50	0	0
	Adam Rolland, Esq. advocate, in annual donations from 1796, and a legacy	752	0	0
1821	James Kettle, writer	30	0	0
	Alexander M'Laren, stabler	50	0	0
	Mrs. Ross, widow of Robert Ross, music-seller	30	11	9
	Mrs. Simpson of Viewfield	285	14	0
1822	Alexander Duncan, Esq. W.S.	200	0	0
	Miss Isabella Hutton of Slyhouses	50	0	0
	Miss Græme	10	0	0
1823	James Anthony, tailor	18	8	8
	Mr. ———— Kay, architect, Edinr.	218	0	0
	Mrs. Cockburn	27	0	0
	Mr. Alexr. Laing, architect, Edinr.	30	0	0
1824	Sum awarded by the Barons of Exchequer	100	0	0
	Thomas Dott, builder	198	0	0
	Miss Chapman	10	0	0
	Alexander Callender, Falkirk	200	0	0
1825	The Directors of the musical festival	50	0	0
	Thomas Cockburn	15	14	0
	William Dick	135	10	9
	William Pelson	143	13	9
	Alexander Fortune, late of India	86	5	0
	Sir William Forbes, Bart.	21	0	0
1828	———— Aitken	100	0	0
	Miss Elizabeth Bonar	20	0	0
	———— Stewart	10	0	0
	Mrs. Ross, Jamaica, (received at various times,)	7452	12	5
1829	Miss Hood	100	0	0
1830	James Douglas, Balnafee	10	0	0
	Mr. M'Gibbon of Greenyards	300	0	0
	Alexander Hutchison	450	0	0
1831	William Thomson, Esq. of Westbarns	500	0	0
	Mrs. Elizabeth Muir	231	6	11
1832	John Tawse, Esq. of Stobshiells	25	0	0
	George Fulton, teacher	30	0	0
1833	The Barons of Exchequer, from vacant stipends, and Mercer's estate	26	4	11
	Francis Ronaldson, Post Office	17	3	0

No. V.

INSCRIPTION ON THE TABLET IN THE SCHOOL-ROOM, ORPHAN HOSPITAL.

SACRED TO THE MEMORY

OF

WILLIAM PEEBLES

Forty-eight years Master of the Orphan Hospital.

Possessing talents which might have fitted him for a higher station,
and
Distinguished by the most unaffected and ardent piety,
He devoted his life and labours
To the instruction and management of the Orphan Children
Educated in this house,
Their father, their counsellor, their companion.
His unassuming modesty, salutary admonitions, and winning manners
Irresistibly gained and secured their affections,
and,
Sanctified by his faith, his example, and his prayers,
Proved the means of leading not a few of them
Into the paths of holiness and peace.
During a lingering illness and under the most acute bodily pain,
That gospel which had been the guide and joy of his life
Eminently supported and cheered his mind
With the resignation of faith and the patience of hope,
Till April 15, 1807, in the 89th year of his age,
He fell asleep in the Lord.
In paying this tribute of respect to the memory
of Mr. Peebles,
The Managers and Corporation of the Orphan Hospital
Wish to present his character
To themselves, to their successors, to the teachers, and to the Orphans,
as an example of
Christian excellence, fidelity, and usefulness
Worthy of their perpetual gratitude and imitation.

" The righteous shall be had in everlasting remembrance."

No. VI.

CLERGYMEN WHO HAVE PREACHED THE ANNIVERSARY SERMONS.

1774 Dr John Erskine, Edinburgh
1775 Mr Robert Walker, do.
1776 Mr Thomas Randall, Stirling
1777 Mr John Kemp, Edinburgh
1778 Dr David Johnstone, Leith
1779
1780 Dr Andrew Hunter, Edinburgh
1781 Sir Henry Moncreiff Wellwood, St. Cuthbert's
1782 Mr William Paul, Newbattle
1783 Dr. Main
1784 Mr William Gloag, Edinburgh
1785 Mr James Brown, do
1786 Mr William Greenfield, do
1787 Mr William Moodie, do.
1788 Dr George Hill, St. Andrews
1789 Dr George H. Baird, Edinburgh
1790 Mr James Brown, Newbattle
1791 Mr Thomas Macknight, Leith
1792 Dr Thomas Hardie, Edinburgh
1793 Mr James Finlayson, do.
1794 Mr Henry D. Hill, North Berwick
1795 Mr Robert Walker, Canongate
1796 Mr Walter Buchanan, do
1797 Mr David Black, Edinburgh
1798 Dr Robert Lorimer, Haddington
1799 Mr Archibald Bonar, Cramond
1800 Dr Andrew Brown, Edinburgh
1801 Mr William Bennet, Duddingston
1802 Mr Robert Balfour, Glasgow
1803 Mr Robert Anderson, Edinburgh
1804 Dr John Thomson, do.
1805 Dr Alexander Brunton, do
1806 Mr David Dickson, St. Cuthbert's
1807 Dr John Campbell, Edinburgh
1808 Dr Thomas Fleming, do.
1809 Dr James Robertson, Leith
1810 Mr Andrew Thomson, Edinburgh
1811 Dr David Ritchie, do.
1812 Mr David Dickson. do.
1813 Mr Walter F. Ireland, Leith
1814 Mr Henry Grey, St Cuthbert's Chapel
1815 Mr Walter Tait, Edinburgh
1816 Mr Angus Makellar, Pencaitland
1817 Dr Andrew Grant, Edinburgh

1818 Dr Thomas Fleming, Edinburgh
1819 Sir Henry Moncreiff Wellwood, St. Cuthbert's
1820 Dr George Muirhead, Cramond
1821 Dr Andrew Thomson, Edinburgh
1822 Dr John Lee, Canongate
1823 Dr George Wright, Stirling
1824 Dr Robert Gordon, Hope Park Chapel
1825 Dr William Muir, Edinburgh
1826 Mr James Henderson, Stockbridge Chapel
1827 Mr John Purves, Lady Glenorchy's Chapel
1828 Mr John Forbes, Hope Park Chapel
1829 Mr James Marshall, Edinburgh
1830 Mr James Martin, Stockbridge Chapel
1831 Mr James Begg, Lady Glenorchy's Chapel
1832 Mr William Scott Moncrieff, Penicuik

No. VII.

OFFICE BEARERS.

Preses of the Incorporation.

1734 Lord Monzie
1751 The Earl of Hopetoun
1752 Sir Gilbert Elliot of Stobs
1764 Alexander Arbuthnot of Knox
1765 Lord Auchinleck
1777 Lord Hope
1778 The Earl of Hopetoun
1816 The Lord Chief Baron Dundas
1819 The Lord President Hope.

Treasurer.

1733 Andrew Gairdner
1739 Thomas Gairdner
1745 William Braidwood
1764 William Govan
1772 Robert Scott Moncrieff
1781 Thomas Tod
1796 Alexander Bonar
1807 David Thomson
—— William M'Lean
1822 Francis Nalder
1828 Robert Paul

Accountant.

1733 Alexander Chalmers
1736 Alexander Meason
1760 Walter Cosser
1779 Christopher Mowbray
1813 William Scott Moncrieff

Comptroller.

1733 James Young
1735 Robert Montgomerie
1736 George Miller
1739 Robert Tod
1740 Archibald Cockburn
1744 Archibald Wallace
1745 Thomas Gairdner
1750 Archibald Wallace
1769 William Galloway
1800 William M'Lean
1807 William Patison
1832 John Tawse

Clerk.

1733 John Louthian
1763 Andrew Stevenson
1771 James Forrest
1783 James Forrest and James Jollie
1787 James Jollie
1817 James and Walter Jollie

Surgeon.

1733 James Dundas
1754 John Boswell
1761 David Wardrop
1793 James Clark
1798 James Bryce
1826 William Brown.

Master.

1733 George Brown
1741 Francis Archibald
1743 John Johnston
1759 William Peebles
1807 Alexander M'Gruar
1808 Alexander Aitken
1810 John M'Donald
1813 James Smith
1815 James M'Culloch
1833 John Ritchie

Matron.
1733 ———Brown
1740 Isobel Paterson
1751 Mary Barless
1771 Margaret Graham
1799 Christian Muckle
1805 Christian M'Lean
1824 Henrietta Burrell.
1833 Janet Sinclair

Female Teacher.
1824 Janet Sinclair.
1833 Jane Panton

Check Out More Titles From HardPress Classics Series In this collection we are offering thousands of classic and hard to find books. This series spans a vast array of subjects — so you are bound to find something of interest to enjoy reading and learning about.

Subjects:
Architecture
Art
Biography & Autobiography
Body, Mind &Spirit
Children & Young Adult
Dramas
Education
Fiction
History
Language Arts & Disciplines
Law
Literary Collections
Music
Poetry
Psychology
Science
…and many more.

Visit us at www.hardpress.net